Peter Taylor Forsyth

Rome, Reform and Reaction

Four Lectures on the Religious Situation

Peter Taylor Forsyth

Rome, Reform and Reaction
Four Lectures on the Religious Situation

ISBN/EAN: 9783744778565

Printed in Europe, USA, Canada, Australia, Japan

Cover: Foto ©Lupo / pixelio.de

More available books at **www.hansebooks.com**

ROME, REFORM AND REACTION

Four Lectures on the Religious Situation; by P. T. FORSYTH, M.A., D.D. Cambridge

LONDON: HODDER AND
STOUGHTON 27
PATERNOSTER ROW 899

Butler and Tanner, The Selwood Printing Works, Frome, and London

To

Rev. Dr. AMORY H. BRADFORD

Montclair, New Jersey

My dear Bradford,—

It has been my happiness to know quite a group of friends with a special genius—"the genius of being beloved." Some are on your side, some on ours; some are now *jenseits*, some are *diesseits* still; one at least I have at home; and one, so near and yet so far, in you. Other men well praise your gifts, or your lineage; have I leave to adorn with *you* the front of this little book?

It appears just after a first and memorable visit to your most hospitable shores, in circumstances which move many besides me to say, "Now in Christ Jesus we who sometimes were far off are made nigh by the blood of Christ." So for these discourses, as for all the Churches, be this the common and hospitable text, however understood in detail.

Always yours,

P. T. FORSYTH

Cambridge, *November*, 1899

Preface

THIS book is not a treatise, but the publication of a Series of Lectures; which may account for the lack of references, some repetition, and some conversational or dogmatic symptoms of direct address. At the same time additions have been made, or parts retained which were omitted in delivery as being in a style adapted for the reader rather than for the hearer.

I ought also to say that, as I do not aim at any contribution of scientific value, I have abstained from reading the recent works of Dr. Fairbairn and Dr. Brown till I am now set free for that pleasure. That they are inimitable would not prevent their being too contagious for the individuality of a comparative amateur on the same topic. And any coincidences that occur may thus mean the more.

Page 170 is based on a passage in Eucken ; and the series on page 45 is a reminiscence from Bunsen.

I am under much obligation to Rev. J. A. Hamilton, of Penzance, for amendments in proof.

Contents

PAGE

LECTURE I

WHAT IS THE REAL NATURE OF THE PRESENT ISSUE ? 13

LECTURE II

WHERE DO WE REALLY GO WHEN WE GO BEHIND THE REFORMATION ? . . . 75

LECTURE III

WHAT DID LUTHER REALLY DO ? . . 113

LECTURE IV

PART I. THE REAL NATURE OF THE PRIESTHOOD 177

PART II. SOME REAL SOURCES OF THE PRIEST'S WELCOME 212

THE REAL NATURE OF THE PRESENT ISSUE

I
THE REAL NATURE OF THE PRESENT ISSUE

I

I DO not share the repugnance felt by a large number of people, especially in the present day, to religious controversy. The ruling spirit of the great classic ages and figures of faith has been one of controversy however rarefied. It is true that it rested always on a deep certainty and peace, but it was a security that did not allow them to become quietists, but thrust them into the front of battle. We have room and need for the men of peace, but one should protest against a tendency to erect them into the ideal figures of Christianity. They deserve love and honour, but in critical times it is other men and other helps that we chiefly need. In a crisis the man of peace may be counted in the main as a friend of the established side. The prophets of the Old Testament were men of war. The whole mission of Israel was to be fulfilled in the face of a gainsaying world. The work of Christ was incessant controversy—the Lord's controversy. The life of Paul was ceaseless warfare. The Epistles of John proceed from the thick of a battle which Christian faith was waging for its life, when Christian love knew how to hate and fear. The great figures of Church history have been those whose words and deeds come down to us from the midst of campaigns. Athanasius, who saved the Church's life, was set against a world in arms. And the Reformation age meant war. Luther lived and breathed in it. If the Reformation is not yet done we must dread war less. It is easy for us to talk against controversy when it is the life-toil of the great controversialists that has given us the ease we propose only to enjoy. We need to revive some of the heroic features of faith. We are in danger from its feminine and sympathetic side, from its restful and acquiescent mood. We are apt to treat religion as the region of ease as well as the secret of peace. We deprecate the opening of its questions, or, when they are opened, the pursuit of them. We do not reflect that no frame of ours could be better than that for the enemies of faith. They are quite willing that we should cultivate a quietist's peace, minimise differences, and dwell on the common stock of belief, so long as we leave them with the monopolies and the abuses they represent. There are many people who think that the kingdom of heaven means first a quiet life and the cultivation of friendly feeling all round. They do not naturally like conflict, and religion is not strong enough in them to compel them beyond their natural likes. They do not reflect that conflict comes to the great warriors not as a sport or hobby, but as a painful duty and a stern obedience. Let them read Jeremiah, the gentle, peace-loving man whom the hand of God thrust into the caldron of his seething time. Let them note in many another how the trumpet broke upon their selfish peace as the breath of God to save them from the stagnation of goodness, and stir them with the tonic of the fight. I am sure that many a time the revival of religion which we pray for ought to come by a renewal of the heroic vein of faith, with a new crusade; and the baptism of the spirit should be a baptism of blood.

One reason why controversy is deprecated at present is that sympathy has been growing at the expense of principle. Our philanthropic energies have, for the time, submerged our energies of righteousness. I do not say so in a grudging spirit. We move forward with one foot at a time. For the present it is the turn of the heart side; but the time is far spent, and it grows needful that, if we are to keep from falling, there should be a step by the other foot and a movement of the other side. It is time that we returned with our attention to the side of mind and principle, that we recognised another test than beneficence, and that we sought to clear our views for action on some of the great old issues now in abeyance. There are whole sections of the public whose mawkish religion needs more than anything else a gospel of severity, others whose sickly charity is anæmic for want of the breath of justice, and others whose æsthetic decorum can only be roused by some action in sufficiently bad taste to break their idol.

There is another reason for that distaste of controversy which takes so much virility from our faith and age.

I do not now mean the dislike of many for the passions which controversy lets loose. People who habitually cannot control their tempers and their tongues should not enter controversy. They are unfit for the heroic and the noble side of life. But, (I may interject,) those also are unfit for it, and are guilty of some cowardice, who give way to the bullies, or who shrink from the advocacy of the right because the enemy uses poisoned arrows. There is a worse thing than the temper and abuse of controversy, and that is the mawkish sweetness and maudlin piety of the people who are everybody's brothers and can stand up to none.

But I leave that and return to the weightier reason

that I have hinted for the dislike of controversy. It is the feeling on the part of many that it is sterile, and leaves us at the end no farther than when we began.

Now this is not the case. I will venture to say that none ever came out of a real argument other than the better for it, provided that they behaved themselves. If they did nothing else, they cleared up their own views to themselves. They probably suggested new aspects of the case to the bystanders. And they may even have done so to their adversary, or he to them. And in any case their faculties were stirred ; their mind was the healthier for the gymnastic ; and they escaped for a time from the women's quarters, and from the office and from the shop, into the breeze. They are not where they were at the outset.

And so it is with the great controversies that mark and make history, and especially the history of the Church. They do not come upon us to-day with exactly the same call, the same problem, the same historic situation as those of our fathers. The problem moves. It does not present itself to us in the fixed formula of our predecessors. It is really a new problem ; it is a new question set in the same rule. Those who handled it before renewed it in *their* time. They added something to it. They passed it on to us as something different, and ready for our contribution through theirs. The people who enlarge most on the sterility of controversy are those who know least about it, who have gone no deeper than its surface, who have resented the call to think, and be just ; or who ran away to save their nice manners as soon as the bad language began. It is a trait of the whole Agnostic habit of mind thus to belittle the past, to succumb to helplessness, and acquiesce in despair. The same habit which says we can know nothing about God says also that we can know nothing about any of those tough and fascinating matters which men have argued for generations. It is the same shallow impatience on both heads, the same scepticism of human effort and intelligence. The same quality of mind as distrusts God's effort in revelation, distrusts man's effort in understanding it. Give us the man that cannot take his mind off the North Pole. The great problems are not to be settled in a generation ; they are of historic dimensions. They extend over many generations, as some mathematical problems may cover days. But each day contributes something to the huge chain of calculation ; and so it is with the great controversies of the past. We take them up where our predecessors left them, not where they found them. There are questions that have lasted or even slept for centuries, and whose aspect is materially and for ever changed by the work of the last fifty years. But it is the change of evolution, not of the kaleidoscope. It moves for all that.

Take the Protestant question. What did the Reformation do? Simply add one to the many efforts at reform already made? No. It attacked the same question, but in quite a new way, with new light from Luther's original experience and genius. But was Luther's experience so new? Again, no. It was the revival of the same controversy as engrossed the life of Paul. It was fighting the same battle over again. But is that not rather hopeless? Surely no, still. It was on a far wider scale, in a far more searching spirit, at least as far as the enemy was concerned. It was a war with Paganism, but it was with the more terrible Christian Paganism. And, besides, *is* it hopeless to find that the great cause which had gone out of clear sight for 1,500 years refused to lie dead, and asserted itself with such amazing power? Is it hopeless to-day to see so much of the work of the Reformation still to be done? We should not find it so. The corruptions and abuses of fifteen centuries were not to be thrown off in one, and it is eighteen centuries that we are struggling with to-day. Was it likely that Europe could speedily get rid of the moral and spiritual malaria which had lain so long in her system that death grew her habit of life? Nay, was it not probable that there should be relapses, that the new life should have a tough fight for it, that it should have to be nursed back through a tedious convalescence, with much to dishearten and much to try us? How often the convalescence is longer than the disease! Again, how vast the Reformation principle is, the evangelical principle! It *is* the Gospel. That is why human nature hates and resists it worse than it does Rome. For long the New Testament principle will not leaven Europe, though it has been 2,000 years at work on it; and the Reformation has been working only a few centuries. The situation is anything but hopeless if we will take pains to understand the nature of the principles at work, of the Gospel, and of the enemy. The hopeless people are the people who will not take pains, who are not in earnest.

If, indeed, our Protestantism to-day called upon us to go back to the Reformers and adopt their beliefs and practices in a mass, we might well demur; and we might suspect the uses of controversy, or its progress in history. But controversy, the battle of truth and right, cannot be the one thing which does not progress amid all the energies of man. And we are not asked to adopt the theology of the Reformers nor their polity *en bloc*. What we are asked to do is to take their principle and carry it out in a way they could not do, to develop the Reformation, to reform the Reformers, to take the results their principle has achieved, to go back with these results upon their positions, to re-read their positions in the light of their own results, to apply these principles afresh to the ground that they themselves have cleared, and so to carry them forward to new conquests and new expressions. Protestantism is not resuming the entire theology of the Reformers, but correcting their theology, when necessary, by their Gospel, by their principle of faith. We may correct Luther's dogmas by Luther's thoughts, and his thoughts by his faith. And so, even the High Church movement of to-day, medieval as it is, is not a mere copy; it is not a return to medievalism in the sense of lifting over bodily the theological contents of the Middle Ages, and pressing them upon faith as if no water had flowed under the bridge from that day to this. It is recalling the medieval principle of the Church, or of faith, and reading the world of to-day in that light. The very Church of Rome itself, with its claim to be the *living* Church, takes stand on a great doctrine of development; and it put the crown on the long series by the doctrine of papal infallibility, which was not formulated till twenty years ago. People speak and write of a Reformation Settlement. There was no such thing. For this country at least the Reformation was much more of an unsettlement. It was a beginning, not an end. It was but the thin end of the evangelical idea which pierces to the dividing asunder of every mere Catholic institution, and must overturn till He come whose right it is to reign directly in each soul. There was nothing in the nature of the Reformation which promised immediate finality either to Church or to State. As a matter of fact it has brought much more ferment than finality, and the more outward ferment in proportion as it gave the soul an inward finality. The peace of the justified waged but the keener war against things unjustifiable. And if the political settlement had been a much more explicit thing than it was, it would still be at the mercy of the principle of spiritual power and freedom which the Reformation only introduced.

It is a great thing to be involved in these noble old controversies. There are many worse things than war on those lofty planes. The object of faith is not to provide us with a quiet life. Little men may belittle any conflict, but the conflict is great. The issue is high. Let it be handled in a high-minded way. Do not let us fight as if our one foe were some village cleric, some rural autocrat, and petty priest. The conflict is one which has engrossed the very greatest human souls and involves the greatest divine destinies. It is not English, but ecumenical. No State question approaches in moment the gravity of the question about the true nature of faith, and the consequent true nature of the Church. It is the human question. It is a war of angels, saints, apostles, prophets; let us wage it as men of the saintly and apostolic faith in Jesus Christ.

II

There are many who reel disheartened in the present religious situation because it appears to them that we are in danger of losing all that the last 300 years have gained, and of having to fight the whole Reformation battle over again. This is not so. Even if the conflict become more severe than it is, it is yet not the old straw that is threshed nor the long dead that is slain. It is indeed the old problem that confronts us; it is not a new one. But it is the old problem at quite a new stage. It is the old problem at a stage which has developed a new answer, or compels the answer in new terms. It is the old problem of the unfinished Reformation; but it has advanced to a stage at which it becomes clear as it never was in its history before that the first answer is Disestablishment. That is the social consummation of the spiritual necessity in the Reformation. The battle with the world for a free Gospel can only be won by a free Church; and a free Church is the inevitable effect of a free Gospel, of the freedom of the spiritual power. At the English Reformation there were but the two alternatives—a royal Church or a Roman Church, Erastianism or Catholicism. If you resented the royal supremacy you could realise the freedom of the Church only in a Catholic form, and between Henry and More our heart is all with More. But history has developed a better way. Before the Reformation the freedom of the State had only been attained by the subjection of the Church, or the freedom of the Church by the subjection of the State. But the existence of the Free Churches has shown, and their prosperity points, another and a better way. The solution of the old problem is a free Church in a free State.

It is the old problem, but it is in a stage quite new. And this means a new stage also in the development of the idea of faith, in the public idea o religion.

Let me explain what I mean. And let me do so by referring first to the history of this country alone, and next to the larger history of the Christian Church.

First as to this country alone.

There have been three great junctures at which English religion has been brought into direct and critical relation with the State. The first was at the

Reformation, the second was at the Commonwealth, and we are in the midst of the third. In the first the spiritual power was completely subjected to the temporal through the passion and self-will of the Tudors, and especially of Henry VIII. In the second it was partially released through the magnificent statesmanship of Cromwell. In the third the release promises to become complete. In the first stage the ruling idea for the Church was still uniformity, only with a lay head instead of a clerical, with Henry where the Pope had been. In the second the ruling idea was toleration, or comprehension, with a tenderness for some form of concurrent establishment. By the providence of God the sects had arisen ; and this, which is so often deplored in connection with Protestantism, became the means by which the idea of toleration was forced upon the public as a step to something higher—religious liberty. In the third stage the ruling idea has passed beyond either comprehension or toleration, yea, beyond liberty ; for the Free Churches are not only let alone by the State, but equally respected, and not only tolerated by each other but owned and acknowledged as members of each other. And it becomes clear that this consummation is only possible throughout by total disestablishment. We regain, on a far higher and more spiritual plane, the freedom which the Church had, and always demands, in the Roman system. It is the old problem of the Church's freedom, but it is in quite a new stage; and it is in a new direction that we look for the solution. For long the only escape from a State uniformity seemed to be into the Roman supremacy; but the last 250 years have opened a new and living way—the way pointed by Independency and heralded in the Commonwealth—the way of the Free Churches, of federated instead of monarchical unity in the Church. This freedom of the Church is the only true completion of the Reformation on its ecclesiastical side. And the reason why the Low Church party are powerless against the priest to-day is because no Established Church can ever in spirit be truly Protestant. It is too institutional, too legal. It is weak against the priest because it is spiritually lamed by its compromise with the State. The Reformation faith that should fight the priest has one hand occupied in clinging to the State and it can do little more than shake the other. Among the crucial religious junctures I did not name the great Evangelical movement of a century ago, which in the Low Church party has now settled on its lees. And I avoided doing so because it neither had nor led to any direct action on the State. It lost the imperial interests of religion. The indirect public and social service of that movement, especially outside the Established Church, has been unspeakable ; but its tendency has never been to the larger historic issues which are most critical for the national life. Its strength and its weakness have been its individualism and pietism. The weakness has been especially developed in the established section of it. And its distaste for public and historic affairs has led to a mental cramp which is another aspect or source of its powerlessness in the present crisis. Whatever may be said of the High Church party, it cannot be said that they have disowned the public, social and historic mind. And nothing could furnish a greater contrast with the fate of the Evangelical party in the Church than the career which the same movement has followed in the Methodist bodies that carried it outside the State. The Reformation principle *found* itself in them ; and it moves in them still with growing power to its true effect of freedom.

III

But why has the course of the Reformation in this country been so slow ? And why have we still to be working out what other lands have long settled ? And why does the conflict spread over not only so many battles but so many campaigns ?

Because the Reformation, though spiritual in its aim and genius, was in this country only to an inferior degree a religious movement. It was in the first place a political movement, and in its methods violent and coercive. It has been cursed with the taint of force, and it has only been slowly purified into a better mind.

There is a striking analogy offered here with the course of spiritual progress in the history of another intractable people, Israel. The soul of the Reformation is the moral spirit of the prophet rising up against the canonical temper of the priest. Now in the history of Hebrew prophetism we have the same course of error and the like correction of it. We have the reforming prophetic spirit in Abijah, Elijah, and all the early prophets, protesting against the pagan or curial corruption of religion, but mixing itself with political conspiracy, and employing political methods even to the extent of massacre and other violent means, as in the case of the priests of Baal. And we have this violence reproducing violence through some centuries, till the kingdom was destroyed by the nemesis of its reactions in the exile. But all the time the prophetic spirit was disengaging itself from this crudity and barbarity of its early methods. It became by experience spiritualised into the almost Christian inspiration of Jeremiah and the second Isaiah. These may be said to have been the persecuted Nonconformists who both carried on the principles and refined the methods of the rugged puritans who went before them and brought to pass the great kingdom to come.

It was a like discipline that passed upon the Protestant movement, in this country at least. As it went on it deepened in its principle and sweetened in its ways. The bane of Henry's action was its violence, its self-will, its mere national and individual passion. In the matter of the divorce there is no doubt the Pope was right and Henry wrong. Had the movement been only of man Henry would have killed it. As it was he threw it back indefinitely, and entailed upon a long posterity the task of making good the errors of his coarse lead. If England had only had but one commanding religious genius to be for her what Luther, Calvin, and Knox were to their respective lands! The like masterful and violent policy marked Elizabeth, though to a less degree. And it was largely compelled, I must admit, by the fight for national life against the incessant political plots and treacheries of Rome. It was the potsherds of the earth striving with the potsherds of the earth by earthy methods on either side.

The Anglicans insist that the Established Church is not a Protestant Church, and there is a sense in which they are right. What established the National Church did not establish the Reformation. That was done by the Puritans, whose tradition we continue.

The National Church was established by Henry, and Henry was no Protestant. The nationalism of the Church had been *founded* before, amid the national aspirations which fermented in the whole of Europe before the Reformation, but it had striven in vain to *establish* itself against the Ultramontanism of the Pope. What did establish it was Henry's act in a plea where Henry was wrong and the Pope was right. The National Church was *established by* (I do not say *founded on*) a crime of wrong and force. And of that crime the Free Churches with their sufferings are the remote expiation, as they are the perfecting of the true and living word of the Reformation.

But the Reformation would have come, Henry or none, though it would have come otherwise and better without the Tudors.

Among the despised and persecuted sects there was growing up a new idea of the Church and its freedom. And when Cromwell came to power—far more truly than Henry the Defender of the Faith—there emerged into political practice for the first time the idea of toleration and mutual respect between the sections of the Church. This idea, with its blossom of civil and especially religious liberty, has been the great direct contribution of Independency to the higher life of England. It was an idea that seemed to many at the time a political peril and a religious crime. It could have come, historically speaking, by no other way than by the sects. They were there by the will of God for the service of His great Church and its freedom. They came to give the idea of spiritual freedom a new interpretation. It was by the descent of this idea under Henry's royal supremacy, and its disguise under the extravagance of the sects—it was through such humiliation, death and burial that the idea passed out of its Roman form and rose into the large liberty of the Spirit for which the Free Churches stand.

But the Commonwealth only placed this idea in a monumental way on the political ground. It was not able to keep it there. The advance was too great and rapid to be permanent. The whole spiritual resource of English Protestantism was expended on this immense move, and there was none left to consolidate it. The great wave swept back; the Restoration came with its disastrous results to morals as well as faith. And it was not till 1688 that the principle of toleration was really incorporated with the English Constitution. And it has taken all the time from then till now to develop toleration into its true form of liberty. The work is not yet complete, but completion is in sight. And the total separation of Church and State becomes to an increasing number not only the solution of present difficulties, but the necessary consummation of our national and ecclesiastical past.

Why was it that the great spiritual triumph of the Commonwealth was so short-lived ? Just because it was (through the inevitable circumstances of the time) to so large an extent unspiritual ; because, though it was the triumph of England's best soul, it was the victory of an army. It was a victory of the stalwarts rather than of the saints. It was faith, but it was mailed faith, faith working by force and secured by the sword. Why has the battle of spiritual liberty been so slow and hard from then to now ? Because of that memory of an army's triumph, though it was the godliest army that the world ever saw, the first serious attempt to make the Bible instead of the Church the ruling influence in State affairs. So bitter were the memories left by that victory that it is doubtful if we should have got even the toleration of a century later had Dissent not become so weak in the reaction as to be thought contemptible and harmless.

Both in Henry's work and in Cromwell's the great triumph was really retarded by the force and haste of the particular victories. He that believeth should not make haste. It was on no national conversion or conviction that either movement stood ; and the wrath of man, even of godly men, does not work out to its high end the spiritual righteousness of God. Spiritual freedom can only be secured by spiritual and reasonable ways. Neither man nor nation can be coerced into freedom. It must sink into men's minds as a principle. It must convert the nation, and not merely the *élite* of the nation, to its faith. A godless king goes down before a godly army. But even the godly army melts before the slow growth and instinct of parliamentary rule. Representative conviction wins permanent victories and achieves beneficent revolutions which are refused to dictatorial conviction. A parliament is *in its nature* a more spiritual thing than a despot, even a godly despot. It appeals to moral conviction and rational consent. It is better that a Church should be ruled by a parliament than by a king. It is better because it is more hopeful. There is more hope that a parliament, with its base deep and deepening in the national reason, should see its true relation to an institution like the Church, which appeals to spiritual conviction alone. There is hope, I say, that a parliament will perceive that its true relation to the Church lies in letting it alone. It may be brought, without a king's loss of *amour propre*, to feel that to sever with the Church is not to part with it or renounce it, but is the debt and honour due to the Church's holier freedom. Severance here means reverence. First the monarch dictates to the Church, then parliament patronises it. We have now come to a point at which both royal supremacy and parliamentary patronage are felt to be unspiritual things, partaking in different degrees of force and earth, compared with the pure spiritual and rational appeal made by the Gospel, which is the charter of the Church's life.

Slowly the conditions of spiritual freedom have been learned, both for the soul and for the Church; and in England most slowly of all Reformed lands. They seem to have been free-born, while with a great price she gains her freedom. While other Churches have been developing their Reformation, we seem only to have been securing it. We have been spending, on the effort to keep from slipping back, the strength that might have carried us far forward. The State with us has gained more from the Church than the Church has from the State. It is a Church whose spirit savours more of the throne than of the Cross, of English pride than Christian penitence. Our overwhelming political genius has brought us, along with untold blessing and glory, also peril and loss. It has yielded to the self-confidence of strength, and attacked questions where even an English statesman must be foiled if he is statesman and no more. Of these questions the chief is that of the Church. For its problems and its freedom the wisdom of this world is nought. The wise have not its secret, and the mighty have not its power, and the mere freeman has not its liberty. Religious liberty brings civil, but civil does not bring religious. And no freedom worthy of the Church can rest upon any methods, political or social, which despise, boycott, or coerce, but only on those which persuade the reason and win our trust. We have learnt this politically; when the lesson has been learnt socially as well, then the true Church will be free in a free State, and faith will be, as the Reformation preached it, its own advocate, patron, defence, and power. As toleration took the place of uniformity, and as liberty grew out of toleration, so out of liberty grows the true fraternity of the Churches, their mutual need and acknowledgment of each other; and thus the federal fabric grows into a holy temple in the Lord.

It is the old long problem, but it is in a new stage. That is so, I have shown, in the evolving history of our own land. May I now move to a wider field, and show that it is so on the scale of Europe and the Church universal?

IV

It will help us to realise the situation on the large historic European scale if we put it in this way. We are familiar with the part played in the history of this country by King, Lords, and Commons. We understand more or less of the way in which their conflicts represent the struggle of the three political principles—

the monarchical, the aristocratic, and the democratic. We see how the interaction of prince, peer, and people has worked out the line of progress. We see how the Commons mastered the King in the fate of the Stuarts, how they are now pressing for a similar mastery of the Lords. We see how the democratic principle swallowed up the monarchical, how it is swallowing up the aristocratic, and how in our American daughter it disposed both of the monarch and the peer. I am saying nothing of the merits of the case. I am simply noting the facts. And I do so in order to mark the same conflict of ideas in the medieval Church, in the Catholicism of the pre-Reformation age. You have the same three principles in collision, the same struggle waged on a continental scale and in the spiritual realm. You have the Pope corresponding to the King with his Divine right. You have the bishops corresponding to the barons or peers, with some claim to constitutional freedom. And you have the mass of the laity, who ever since the thirteenth century had been growing in culture, wealth, and municipal freedom. For a long time in this country we had the quarrels of King and barons; and so in the medieval Church it was a long war between the Pope and the bishops. It was a question that became acute in the twelve years' Council of Basle in the fifteenth century, when it was decided by the bishops that a general council was above the Pope, and had the power, on due cause, of deposing him. That marked a memorable stage in the struggle of the Church to save itself from the despotism of the Roman Curia, or what we now call the Vatican. It seemed as if the episcopal principle, the conciliar principle, the House of Lords' principle, were going to save the Church from its despot and its abuses, and reform it so far to the mind of the spirit. It looked as if it would prune the papacy as the barons won our popular rights in Magna Charta from King John. But events were too strong for the council. It could not carry out its principle into fact. The papacy was too strongly fixed for the bishops to dislodge it. The Pope was himself a bishop, and the product of the episcopal system. That system had not the power, the secret, of reforming and saving itself. A century later the Pope was as powerful and mischievous for the Church as ever. The whole Church, its morals and its doctrine, were sacrificed to Rome. To build St. Peter's, Europe was overrun with the scandal of papal indulgences. It was built with human sin and shapen in iniquity.

Meantime there had been coming up in the wake of both Pope and bishop the Commons of the Church, the layman, and especially the monk. I couple these two because they represented for that age the democratic principle. Neither layman nor monk was priest; both Pope and bishop were. And that was why the bishop could not conquer the Pope. Satan could not cast out Satan. Well, behind the struggle of Pope and council there was moving up the democracy (in the form of that day), with a remedy far more drastic than either could bring to bear on the state of things. Pope and bishop were exchanging anathemas, but how was it meanwhile with the third great quantity, the soul—the mad, guilty, lost soul? Pope and prelate were at their long duel, and they were so engrossed with each other that they did not see the crowd of hungry souls that were pressing nearer and nearer round them, asking to be fed with the bread of life, and released from the curse of guilt. Men had turned away from the priests to the monks for some centuries now. Movement after movement had risen to attempt for the great Church that reformation, that emancipation, which the curia would not, and the councils could not, bring about. The devout, the sin-torn, the humane, turned from the altar to the cloister. But, alas! monasticism itself fell a victim to the same corruption, or the same impotence, as paralysed the other organs of the Church. Something was wanting to them all. And it was the Gospel, dealing directly with conscience and guilt. What the sacraments and absolutions of the Church could not do away was sin as guilt upon the conscience and not as a mere infection of our nature; it was sin as guilt and damnation. It was the removal of guilt that the soul cried out for, and that the Church could not give. It was grace as mercy and reconciliation, not as mere amnesty and sweetening of the soul—grace as an act of God on the moral soul itself—that was the only remedy for sin when sin came home as guilt to the conscience. It was grace as a gospel, and not as a mere influence, not as a mere sacramental infusion, that was the one thing needful for the tormented soul. Even monasticism could not supply that.

Yet it was out of monasticism that the real saving word came. It was a monk that saved—I do not say the Church, I say the Gospel, Christianity. The Church is not worth saving, except for the sake of the Gospel. And the Gospel was just what an episcopal, priestly and Catholic Church could not save. Luther was the protagonist of the single sinful soul—the third estate, the supreme interest, of the Church, the first charge on it. *Salus populi suprema lex.* The cause of the democracy is the cause of the soul as conscience; and the Reformation was the moral soul, the conscience, reasserting its place in the Church through the Gospel, in a way unparalleled since the first century.

It is hopeless for Rome, or Anglicanism either, to attempt what they are attempting now—to be the

Church of the democracy. The religious democracy means a moral freedom utterly foreign to Rome, or to any priestly Church. It means a freedom of faith, of conscience, and of person, to which the priesthood is a standing contradiction. What brought these was the Reformation. The Reformation was the moral soul of the people rising against a priestly order that had hopelessly abused its power and always must. Spiritual falsehood *must* end in moral abuse. The Roman priesthood is a spiritual lie, and it is self-doomed to moral wreck and a public reaction. The Reformation for Europe corresponded to the Commonwealth in England. It was in relation to Pope and bishop what the Commonwealth was in relation to King and Lords.

Luther was the Cromwell of the Church; Cromwell was the Luther of the State. The only remedy for the state of things in the Church was the radical movement which in Luther gave the Gospel back to the soul. It remodelled the Church after the pattern shown on the mount of Calvary, by way of redemption, of forgiveness, as a personal experience. The Church could only exist as a community of the forgiven, not merely of the absolved; as a society of priests, and not a priest-led society; as a congregation of the justified, living by their personal faith, and having their spiritual head in Christ alone. The great and cardinal religious principle of the Reformation was connected with sin, and it declared that for the forgiveness of sin the priest was not a necessary party. That is the real issue still. Is the priest essential to forgiveness? We say no, as the Reformers said. The priest was by them swept aside, along with Pope and bishop in so far as these stood upon their magical priesthood as essential between God and man. Forgiveness meant conversion, the direct action of God on the soul and access by the soul to God. And the conversion of the soul was so radical and so central that it carried with it a total change in the constitution of the whole Church. The power that remade the soul was the only power that had right to prescribe the fashion and order of remaking the Church. The Church is but the social expression of the same principle of grace as saves and changes the single soul. The polity of the Church is latent in the principle of our saved experience. So it was in the beginning, in the Church's first making; and so now in this great re-beginning it was declared to be. The Church system, like the Church doctrine, ought by right to be the expression of personal, saving, experimental faith. No constitution was given the Church, even by Christ—no bishops, no priests. His apostles were not officers, but ministers; not ecclesiastics, but preachers. The constitution grew historically, out of the needs and insights of Christian faith, and it became historically corrupt, by the infection of a pagan time. But with this corruption, in priest, or priestly bishop, or Pope, the primitive and germinal faith is always in deadly war. The Spirit leaves the Church where it is compelled into these channels. The Holy Spirit did not of course desert all Romanists, but it did desert the Roman Church in its official organs and its Jesuit policy. The home of the Holy Spirit, of Redemption, and the Gospel was henceforth to be where the word of the Reformation Gospel came with power and effect. Generous Romanists concede to us heretics some workings in individual souls of the uncovenanted mercies of God, but they monopolise for their Church the chief blessing of His perennial corporate guidance. That is just how we put it in respect to Rome. And we do so because we must believe with the New Testament that the Spirit goes with the Gospel, and not with the succession and the sacraments. It is not at home in a Church where we hear more about absolution than about redemption, where devotion is more than conscience, and where the sacraments are more than the living Word.

V

But what was the effect of the Reformation on the old strife within the Roman Church between Pope and bishop, Popes and councils? The effect was what is called the Counter-reformation. The old policy of reforming the Church by councils of Catholic and monarchical bishops was resumed. It is the refuge the Anglican Church is taking to-day. Anglicanism has so far sided with the Counter-reformation. But it was more than reform that the Church really needed. It was conversion, regeneration. And it was regeneration that it received from Luther and his friends. The Regeneration would be a much more fit name than Reformation for a movement which changed central ideas of Christianity like grace and faith, and turned religion from assent into experience, from assent to a Church into experience of a Saviour. But the policy of mere reformation, mere amendment, was the only one of which the debased Church was capable. An institutional Church never knows its own spiritual ineptitude. Mere reform is about all that bishops, or any other officials, *can* do; and they are very slow in doing that till they are pushed on from behind and beneath. The old policy of conciliar reformation, then, was thought adequate and was resumed, and the Council of Trent was called. But councils were not now what they had been. The Reformation had withdrawn from the Roman Church the spirit, the element, that had given the Council of Basle the slow strength it had. The intellect and conscience of Christianity were among the Reformers. What intellects these were! The Roman Church was left without the moral power to vindicate the Church's freedom against the Pope. In the Council of Trent there was not much done to destroy the abuses which caused the Reformation. Little heed was taken of differences within the Roman Church itself; while much was done to controvert the principles of the Protestant heresy. But the serious constitutional feature of the Council of Trent was this, that it surrendered the ground taken by its predecessor of Basle against the Pope. The Vatican came out of it so much stronger than before that the popes frequently afterwards (especially in dealing with Jansenism) took to settling matters of doctrine on their own responsibility. In 1854 Pio Nono raised the doctrine of the Immaculate Conception of Mary to a dogma in this way, without consulting a general council at all. What he had was only a conference of bishops in sympathy. And at last, in 1870, the Council of Rome delivered the whole Church for ever into the hands of the Pope by the dogma of papal infallibility. That was the complete victory of Curialism, of Vaticanism. It was thus for ever proved that general councils are useless without the evangelical element which the priesthood denies and excludes. Councils plus the priesthood must end where the Council of Trent has ended—in the deification of the Pope. This is a lesson which Laud had not learned, and which the High Church Anglicans to-day even do not grasp. This deification of the Pope is the latest act of what has been called "the spiritual tragedy of European society."

The first act of that tragedy was the catholicising of the Church in the second century through the power of the monarchical *Bishop*.

The second act was the consequent secularising of the Church in the fourth century by its association with the throne under Constantine—its debasement by the power of the *Emperor*.

The third act may be said to have been the final adoption at Trent of the theory of Transubstantiation in the mass. It was there and then that the mass was finally defined as a propitiatory sacrifice. It was thus that the awful power of the *priest* was locked about the neck of the Church. The catechism of the Council of Trent describes the priests as gods much more than angels. "Ipsius Dei personam in terris gerunt—quem merito non solum angeli sed dii etiam, quod Dei immortalis vim et numen apud nos teneant, appellantur" (ii. 7, 2).

The fourth act of that tragedy is the promulgation of the dogmas of the Immaculate Conception (the sinlessness) of Mary and of the infallibility of the *Pontiff*. Thus the united power of bishop, emperor and priest was for ever fastened on the Church in a Pope, and its doom and debasement sealed thrice sure.[1]

What will the fifth act be? and how will the dreadful *dénoûment* and crisis come?

Did I say ill when I said that the Holy Spirit of Christ, of the Cross, and of the Gospel, had forsaken the Roman Church as a Church and taken its abode elsewhere?

And is there any hope when the crisis comes but in the evangelised people, in the monarchical democracy of Christ alone, when the divine right of bishop and priest will be slain (as that of king has been slain among us), and they will be there, if there at all, for the service of the Church and not for her rule,

---

[1] Pio Nono was the victim of a self-idolatry which seems hardly sane, and which reminds us of some phases of another career. The German Emperor allows himself to be referred to in an expression like "the Gospel of your sacred majesty." And Pio would use phrases like this, "Keep, my Jesus, the flock which God has committed to Thee and me." He would apply to himself, "I am the way, the truth and the life." He regarded his troubles as a renewal of the sufferings of Christ. One of his cardinals spoke of him in 1866 as the living incarnation of the authority of Christ. Veuillot (1866) identified the crucified of Jerusalem and the crucified of Rome so far as to say to both alike, "I believe in thee, I adore thee." In 1868 the great Catholic newspaper of Rome said, "When the Pope thinks, it is God thinking in him." Faber proposed an act of devotion to the Pope as a supreme test of Christian sanctity. In 1874 a Jesuit paper applied to Pio the words, "Which of you convinceth me of sin?" And there was a hymn sung by the German Catholics celebrating his priestly jubilee in 1869, "Pius, priest, our sinful age, wondering, finds no sin in thee."

as her ministers and not as her lords? Is there any hope for the great Armageddon but in the completion of the Reformation, in the rescue of the Gospel from cultured humanism on the one hand, and from traditional priestism on the other, for the true Church of a faith which is personal experience of forgiveness direct to the soul from Christ in every age?

VI

But to grasp the present situation in the Anglican Church let us go back. We have these two currents in the Church of the sixteenth century—that of the Gospel, by a conversion and regeneration worked through personal faith ; and that of the Church, by a mere reformation, worked through bishops, as Church lawyers and politicians, upon the Church's creed and practice. The one lays all stress upon the Christian's universal priesthood, and consecrates no form of Church government as of divine right ; the other lays all stress on the priesthood of a class and upon an episcopal regime. The one operates by personal faith ; the other throws that into the rear, and is chiefly concerned about the reform of the Church as an institution, and the perfecting of its ritual, by means of councils—councils of men often singularly devoid of the holiness which is the condition of divine knowledge ; councils no more consistent than those of Basle, Trent, and Rome.

Well, is this not just the difference between the Free Churches and the bishops to-day ? On which of these two currents does the Anglican Church of to-day embark ? One of its most brilliant representatives tells us that the chief value of the Reformation was that it called forth the Council of Trent and its blessings to the Church. The chief value of the Gospel was the enhancement of the bishops. The Church of England is a child of the Reformation, but the clergy of England are children of the Counter-reformation in principle and spirit. The inner spirit and temper of Anglicanism is that of a return, more or less prudent, to the method of this Counter-reformation and its conception of truth. Canon MacColl, in his book *The Reformation Settlement*, quotes with approval words which have the imprimatur of Cardinal Manning— "All that we know and believe now, the entire cycle of Christian doctrine in all its circumstances, was known and believed by the apostles on the day of Pentecost before the sun went down." Its faith is in councils of bishops as the organs of Church reform, a repudiation of the lay element, and a depreciation of its supreme and priestly power of faith, a culture of formal reverence and a neglect of the soul, a rehabilitation of the priest and a corresponding trifling with human guilt. The Church is placed in the authoritative, not to say infallible, place which Rome gives to the Pope—the priest-led Church with its episcopal councils.

Observe, besides, the blindness, or the affected blindness, of these counter-reformers. The Council of Trent claimed to be the consummation of a series of reform movements which had been working in the Church quite independent of Protestantism. It simply carried on the Catholic tradition of the Church (that is, the bishops) mending itself. Protestantism was treated as an episode to be ignored in the development of the Church, an excursion which refused to be recalled and so became an excrescence. It could therefore be cut off and dropped without the true Church losing a limb or suffering in beauty. This is really the line taken by Anglicanism to-day. It ignores Nonconformity with its history of at least two centuries and its possession now of more than half the nation. It affects to ignore any contribution from that quarter, though its whole attitude to the country has been changed by it, as Trent was to Europe by the Reformation. As the old counter-reformers ignored the Reformation, so to-day our counterfeit reformers ignore our Re-reformation. (I call them counterfeit reformers because, to effect their ends, they use a position given only to a Protestant

Church.) Anglicanism as a movement stands by the institution rather than the soul. It places itself in the line of Church *reform*, not reformation, not regeneration. The Holy Church never needs regeneration, it says—only reform. Its institutional idea of faith is quite satisfactory. It is self-satisfied. It heals lightly the wound of the daughter of the people. It would only reform upon Trent and recur to Basle. It would discard the supremacy of the Pope and restore that of the episcopate. It would not discard the priest, but only the Jesuits, who have captured the counter-reformation. It rejects the white Pope and the black—the Pontiff at Rome and the General of the Jesuits—but it holds to the bishop and the priest as essential to the Church, and would fain hold to the mass. It goes round the Reformation and catches up the middle age Catholicism, of which it claims to be the true continuity and successor. The Anglican Catholic keeps the medieval idea of religion, or faith, as a threefold cord of knowledge, conduct, and mystic sacraments. He discards that idea of faith which really constitutes a new religion recovered from the New Testament, in which faith is personal trust in a personal Saviour, the soul's direct, experiential, and priestless answer to God's grace as the forgiveness of sin, the destruction of guilt, and reconciliation by the blood of Christ alone.

VII

Our insular issue is the revival of the question of Laud's day, whether the Church of England is Catholic or Evangelical, priestly or lay, whether its Reformation did more than break with the Pope, whether it was religious or institutional, whether it ought not to catch up and work out its religious continuity with the Catholic Church of the Middle Ages after effecting by all the last 300 years no more than the rejection of the Pope, whether the continuity of the Church was in its bishops or in its faith, in what linked Laud with Cyprian or Luther with Paul.[1] But while it is a revival of this question that we see, it is not merely a threshing of old straw. It is being discussed inside the Established Church in another than the spirit of Laud's age. It is more free from political complications and afterthoughts. It is being raised by really religious men—men not, like Laud, of hard, formal, mechanical intelligence— in the interests of the Church far more than of the State, and on Church more than on political principles. It is raised by men to whom the freedom of the Church and its autonomy are dearer than political

---

[1] "Pusey's idea in the *Eirenicon* was to make the Trent decrees a basis of reconciliation; if the Romanists would only confine themselves within Tridentine limits, he hoped to screw up Anglican teaching so far" (Salmon, *Infallibility*, p. 202).

and dynastic schemes, and who are not prepared to pay any and every price for establishment. That is to say, the issue is being raised within the Erastian Establishment on Free Church principles, in a monarchical Church on democratic principles. They are in a false position. In point of principle we agree with the High Churchmen and not with Sir W. Harcourt; but in point of honesty we agree with Sir W. Harcourt and not with them. Still that purer idea of the Church on their part is a great gain and a great encouragement. History is not simply moving in a circle, and a small circle, of a few centuries. It is still the ultimate issues of the Reformation that are being worked out in a new form, in a real spiritual progress. And the same spiritual freedom that has made us to be outside of the Church is making for us inside the Church. For our great object is not the rejection of the Church, but the release of the Church to her own spiritual and autonomous rule. And the great blessing of that will be the restoration of the officer of the Church to his proper place, his elevation from a priest of the sacraments to be a minister of the Word. When the Church is free to be herself, her New Testament self, it will not be so very hard for the Holy Ghost to deal with the priest. If the priest will come out from behind the prestige of our common State we can reach him with the Spirit's weapons of the Gospel. And we are implicitly committed to this as the completion of the *national* and *ecclesiastical* past. First, to complete the *ecclesiastical* past. To complete the Church we must not simply evade the Reformation and fall back on a medieval Catholicism slightly adjusted to this age. We must complete the Reformation because it went behind even Catholicism and rediscovered the faith and Church of the New Testament. The power and right of the Reformation over us is not that it was a new invention, a new idea, but the rediscovery and revelation of the primitive Christian idea and of the New Testament. Of that I may speak later. But, secondly, in pressing on our line we are surely fulfilling the *national* past, and realising the layman's power, faith, as the ruling power in the Church.

Henry's Reformation in throwing off the Pope did more than it knew. It implicitly threw off the priest. The head of the English Church was now a layman, not a cleric. But he was the King. There remained, and still remains, the incubus of the State. The layman must be a believing man. And the beginning of the State's rejection was also through men who were doing more than they knew. The Nonconformists of 1662, it is true, had not our Free Church principles explicitly before all their minds. They came out in protest against the priest and his associations. They were completing the work of those who rejected the Pope. But in throwing off the priest they could only do so by throwing off the State that sheltered the priest. And so they set the foundation of our Free Churchism on an Evangelical base, where indeed all the freedom of the Church lies. A Church free from the State will soon find it cannot be free with the priest. It cannot be free for Christ, and it will proceed to deal with the priest in the light and power of that Gospel which makes it amid all perversions a Church still. These old Nonconformists were not all that we mean by Free Churchmen. They builded better than they knew. The Scotch Free Churchmen of 1843 were not as clear and thorough about Free Church principles as the Free Church has become to-day. Nor did the Evangelical Methodists of last century see where their Evangel was going to take them ecclesiastically. Many of them are not sure about it now; but is there any doubt how it must be? Luther did not foresee the great and searching work he laid his hand to; and I am sure none of the first Christians, not even St. Paul, saw what the ultimate effect of their principles would be on the long history of the world.

So little are these movements due to human device; so much are they the organs of a diviner, all-seeing Spirit, of a principle latent in the perennial Gospel, and bound to overturn, overturn till the Cross take its right and reign.

VIII

The real issue then which is raised in the struggle now going on in the Church of England demands *our* attention because it is really a struggle as to the true nature of Christianity, and especially English Christianity. It is not a question of ritual. It is a far deeper question than one about a more or less of ritual. Nor is it one as to whether Episcopacy is *preferable*; it claims to be *sole*. Nor is it a question of bringing back the Pope or keeping him out. So long as the Pope claims the temporal power, and asserts his place as a continental sovereign, England is inaccessible to him. The national independence of this country will always protect us from a Pope who is not wholly a spiritual power. It is not the sovereign Pope we dread, but the priest Pope. The issue is not between Popery and Protestantism, but between priestism and the Gospel, between sacerdotalism and evangelicalism. The antagonist of the Catholic is not to be described by a word so negative as Protestant, but by the word evangelical. And this drives me into some theology.

When the great breach took place at the Reformation, what was discarded in England, I have said, *was* the supremacy of the Pope. It was Curialism, it was Vaticanism, it was the Italian suzerainty which finally conquered the Catholic Church in 1870. But the European movement was really a greater. It was more than political, more than ecclesiastical; it was religious, it was spiritual. It concerned the way of forgiveness and the place of forgiveness in religion. It had especial reference to the *place* of forgiveness. Was forgiveness itself the Gospel, or only an incident of the Gospel? Was faith faith in forgiveness, or was it faith in something else, say in the love of God, with forgiveness for a mere accident of the position, a clearing of the way, to be forgotten when the path was opened? Does Christian faith begin and abide in forgiveness or only pass through that stage? The conflict concerned the nature of grace and the corresponding nature of faith. The Catholic view of grace is sacramental, the Protestant is evangelical. In the Catholic idea grace is, as it were, a new substance infused into the soul, first by baptism, then by the mass (*gratia infusa*). It is a sort of antiseptic influence made to pervade the spiritual system like new blood. The blood of Christ is understood in a material way, though in the way of a very refined material. It does not give a new righteousness, but power to please God by the old. And the faith that answers it is an acceptance of the Church's power to convey this rarefied and spiritualised substance. The love or charity so produced is thought of in the like way as a sort of spiritual ether infused into the soul. But in the Protestant and evangelical idea grace is not an infusion, but an act and way of God's treatment of us. *It is not infused, but exercised.* It deals with man as a will, not as a substance. It is the same as mercy, the mercy of God, the forgiveness of sin, the cancelling of guilt, the change and not the mere pacifying of the conscience. In a word, for Catholicism grace is magic, for Evangelicalism it is mercy. The grace of Evangelicalism is Christ, the Gospel, the Word. The faith that answers that is living faith in a living person directly in converse with the soul. It is a new type of religion, and not merely a variety of the old. It is faith changed from assent to trust. So the Reformation was a movement affecting not only the hierarchy or polity of the Church, but the whole nature of the Church; it challenged the whole Catholic view of Christianity, the whole Catholic view of salvation. It was not the Pope only that was challenged, but the Catholic and medieval conception of faith, of religion.

From this great searching and fundamental movement even the insularity of England could not be exempt. The greater spirits of the Church were profoundly interested in the large spiritual affairs of the Continent. It is only since the Reformation that England has become the most provincial of all European countries in her thought, most cut off from the stream of European culture, most self-satisfied in her isolation, and most unconscious of her ignorance. Her Reformers and Puritans represented the last of the great cosmopolitan influences on her spiritual culture. At the Reformation England was through the Church a portion of the West still. Her Church had not yet become sectional. It was Catholic and not national. And so the movement of the court and the politicians could not stop with them. To renounce the Pope meant renouncing in principle that Western Catholicism which had borne the Pope for its inevitable fruit. It was renouncing the whole Church of the West. There was more at issue even than the independence of the national Church; there was the independence of the individual soul throughout Christendom. It was a *human* issue, and the greatest.

Like much else in English affairs, that which was really the most vital issue was not the issue that held the foreground in historic time, in the contemporary mind. The movers, I would repeat, did not know all that they were moving. The Reformation in

England (not in Germany) only *began* by renouncing the Pope ; its real nature came later to light—not under Henry VIII., but under Elizabeth. It was the renunciation of the priest. In throwing off the Pope what was really rejected was the priest, though that was not realised at the time. Henry had no idea of such a thing. He was first a devotee of his own passion and self-will. He was next a Catholic nationalist, a Home Ruler, an Anglican Catholic, a defender of the Catholic faith. The vital nerve of Catholicism has two branches—the institutional and the priestly. I speak of the latter first. The former will engage us afterwards. The true inwardness of the Reformation was the rejection of priest and mass. And it was a rejection caused by the return to the Bible and the rediscovery of the Gospel. What dislodged the priest was the Gospel. It was the faith that made every Christian man his own priest in Jesus Christ. The true anti-Catholic movement is not protesting against the Pope, but preaching the Gospel that kills the priest. It is evangelical. The Elizabethan Puritans were the champions of this true and ultimate reformation. It was they who made it what it had been in Luther—a reformation of *religion*. For Henry and his satellites it was but a readjustment of the Church, the change from an Italian to an English head. The Church had been the ecclesiastical counterpart of

European civilization; it was now the ecclesiastical counterpart of the English nation.

The controversy then was really (though not consciously) this: Is a Catholic Church with the priest the true Church of England, or an evangelical Church with the minister who is a layman? Was the ruling power in the Church lay or cleric? It was no question *then* which of two separate *bodies* was the true Church, for there were not two to choose from. The Puritans were still members and believers in a National Church; and there was but the one body, with two tendencies in mighty conflict in its soul. The two bodies came later with the Nonconformists. After this separation caused by the Act of Uniformity there was a long peace of a sort. With the Revolution the Church of England was declared to be Protestant, and the issue raised by the Puritans won both inside and outside the Established Church. But the victory within the Establishment was due chiefly perhaps to political causes, and therefore it was never settled on a religious or final principle. The real religious principle of Protestantism has been in the care of the Nonconformists. The English Prayer Book is a half-baked compromise which is Catholic in its services and Protestant, nay Calvinist, in its articles. The Prayer Book is a cake half turned which deranges the digestion of its Church.

I am ready to grant that in the wisest of the Anglicans there is a modification of the medieval ideas even of the priesthood. They may be willing to regard the priest as the representative of the Church rather than its ruler, as an expression, a projection, of the universal priesthood rather than its creator. Yet so long as they hold to the theory of baptismal regeneration they do practically make the priest the creator of the Church. So long as they cling to the apostolic succession they fatally sever the government of the Church from the living soul of the Church.[1] And the fact that they cling to the name priest, in spite of its studied rejection by the New Testament, shows that they do so because they give the authority and tradition of the Church a place too nearly abreast of Scripture. It is not altogether because priest expresses the sacrificial idea (which is essential to Christianity) in a way that minister does not. But the cardinal defect of their position is still in their conception of religion, that is to say in their ideas of faith and grace. Faith is still for them primarily an institutional thing. It is inseparable from faith in an empirical institution, the Church and its officers. It is not the direct and simple response to grace as an act and mercy of God in Christ through the Gospel to the believing soul. Their Church and priest are absolutely necessary to salvation.

[1] See concluding Lecture.

Their faith is institutional, it is not evangelical. The Gospel for them is not where it should be in price and power above the Church. They do not realise the full force of the fact that it was the Gospel that made the Church, and always must make it. The Church was before the Bible, but it was not before the Gospel, it was not before faith, which is the answer to the Gospel and not to the Church. Such Churchmen have another than the Christian idea of faith, which is evangelical, an answer with the heart to the word of reconciliation, with the conscience to the act of redemption. They do not grasp the fact that the reformation of the Church means at its centre the reformation of faith, the change of the soul; that the Church needs deliverance not only from errors, nor from abuses, but from burdens. And they do not see that their conception of the bishop and of the priest as of the essence of the true Church lays a burden on the Church which it was the business of the Reformation once for all to cast off, not only as an impediment to the Church's working, but as a load of suffocation upon faith itself. This institutionalism lowers the temperature of faith, and it lowers the sense of sin. It sits with a frosty weight of tradition, convention, and worldliness upon the ideals of Christian people. Why is the Church so much less worldly than it should be? It is the place which has been held in the religion of this country by a Church more institutional than evangelical that is responsible for most of the crude and childish moral sense of the Christian public, the lack of Christian as distinct from ecclesiastical enthusiasm, and the want of sensibility in the Christian conscience. Nowhere are these things more deplored than by some Churchmen who fail to see the cause I name. A morality merely conventional and social has blocked the way of a morality inspired and tested by the Cross; and the conscience of thousands has been stunted by the sealing of pagan ethics learned at school with the seal of a Church which for them had replaced the Gospel as the moral authority. The establishment of a Church more institutional than evangelical weights faith too heavily for its purpose in the kingdom of God.

To demand the bishop and the priest in the name of the Gospel is to ask in Christ's name for what Christ never named. It is to load the Gospel with something that neither Christ nor Paul put into it, and to empty it of much that they thought of its essence. It is throwing the weight of the Church into the wrong scale in the age-long issue between Romism and Evangelism. It is to re-introduce upon the Gospel the spirit of the law. It is a perpetuated Judaism. It is the spiritual and fatal restoration of the Jews. It is a Christian anachronism. It is to cherish an idea of faith that the Gospel of the Cross left behind, a Pelagian and Synergistic idea of faith which is fatal to faith in its absolute and imperial sense in the Gospel. It dissolves the work of Paul. It restores the Gospel to the law. A Church established by law can only be a law Church, a statutory Church, a branch of the public service, rather than the conservatory of the public conscience and the home of the godly soul. It becomes another Gospel. The struggle is one for the very nature of Christianity as Gospel and not law. The beginning of all Christian truth, said the Reformers, is to grasp the distinction between law and Gospel. If we could but see that, and fight the battle on that sharp issue, the conflict might be honester and shorter. The battle of the Evangelical Free Churches is for the New Testament idea, the true Christian idea of grace and faith. It is war between faith in an institution and faith in a Gospel, faith to which priest or bishop is essential and faith which is perfect without either. It is for a forgiveness which is complete without the priest, and damaged by him. What we Free Churchmen are committed to is the Reformation in the sense of a rebirth of religion, and not a mere readjustment of the Church. Luther never began with the idea of reconstructing the Church, but with the experience in him of a new conscience, of a new conception of religion, of grace and faith. He was converted from the Church, not from the world. It is not our form of government, our view of history, that is so different from that of our adversaries, but our view of faith, of religion itself, of the soul's relation to Christ, of the meaning of Christ for the soul, of the will and nature of the object of faith—God. Oh, it is a very deep and serious issue that is raised, and so long as the Gospel Word endures it can never be stilled till the Gospel principle come to its own in the Church. And I will freely say that it means a regeneration of faith in the Free Churches no less than in the unfree. For the state of faith and the idea of faith which make Catholicism and its priest possible and fashionable are *our* misfortune and *our* defection as well. We too are infected with that poverty of personal faith and New Testament knowledge which the priesthood thrives on. And I much agree with the fine saying of a great Roman Catholic writer: "When the day of reconciliation comes to the Churches it will start from the confession of our common guilt."

What the Church needs as the condition of reformation is a regeneration of the idea of faith and the consequent humiliation.

IX

To sum up, there are three ways in which the work of the Reformation may be viewed and is viewed to-day. First, there are those who have nothing for it but antagonism and abuse. They think it was a huge historic mistake and calamity for the Church. And they believe that the chief and permanent reform was one which the Reformation brought about against its will and in correction of its work, viz., the reformation which the Catholic Church effected on itself in the Council of Trent. This view is not confined to the Romanists, but is the view of the High Anglican party as expressed in such writings as those of the late Aubrey Moore. Yet it will be noted that there was nothing more central to the Council of Trent than the authority of the Pope.

Secondly, there are those who regard the work of the Reformation as called for in its day but now spent in its effects. The protest was made when it was needful, and it was a real contribution to the history of the Church. But its work is done; the Catholic Church received a lesson it will not easily forget. Many of its abuses were rectified, and with the correction of the abuses the necessity ceased to maintain the protest. The Reformers are now chiefly interesting to the historian, and have no direct or vital meaning for the religious life of the Church. That life, overleaping the Reformation and the abuses that created it, must go back and connect itself with the greater and earlier ages of medieval Catholicism, which again continued the true patristic tradition. The Reformation was thus a temporary expedient for the cure of certain abuses. It may be thanked and pensioned off for its services at a certain juncture, but it must never be allowed to take the reins of Christian progress or turn its course out of Catholic grooves. Perhaps this is the most distinctive Anglican view in so far as it can be reached.

Thirdly, there are those who regard the Reformation not as a temporary movement for the correction of certain abuses, but as a really new point of departure in the history of the Church and a profounder return to the mind of Christ and the New Testament. It was not simply a crisis or Church history, but it was a rediscovery of the vital element in Christianity, which the Church had lost for much more than 1,000 years. It was a return to a more than patristic antiquity—to the New Testament, and in the New Testament to St. Paul. It was more like a Regeneration than a Reformation. Its authors did not intend more than a Reformation of the Church, but what God meant with them was a Regeneration of Christianity. It was upon this line that the true continuity of the Church should for the future succeed. The Reformation was not a loop line bringing us back to Catholicism on a higher plane. It was now to be the main line; and the spiritual traffic of the world was to be diverted from Rome on the old route and sent chiefly by the new track. The real spiritual continuity was from St. Paul by Luther, and not from the fathers by the schoolmen. It was not an ecclesiastical revolt, but a religious crisis, a spiritual new birth of the Church. It is not to be undone, it is not to be antiquated; but it is to be developed. Its principle is to be the vital principle of Christian progress and the most powerful agent on earth of the Kingdom of God. Our Christian business to-day is to complete for the Church that which was given in principle in the creative moment of the Reformation. We have to disentangle it from the relics of Catholicism which it inherited, but which are really incompatible with its principle. And we have to work it clear of the confusions and alloys that clung to its first stage from the state of culture, politics, and society on which it emerged. We have to insist that there is but one object of faith, which is not the Church, and not truth, but the cross of Christ; one mediator between God and man, and one confessor, the priest Christ Jesus; one seat of revelation, which is the Bible; and one principle of revelation, which is the Gospel. We have to go back to the Bible and interpret it by its own inner light of the Gospel, and not by the Church. It is the Bible that interprets the Church, however the Church may expound the Bible.

I need not say that this third view of the Reformation is ours. Christ should be master in His own house. The government of the Church should be in the hands of the Church—not of a dead and gone Church, but of a living Church, as Rome truly says. But, as Rome does not say, it should be in the hands of faith, not of a priesthood—of a believing people. We do not disown the Church, but we reduce the Church to its proper place for the Kingdom as prescribed by the nature of the Gospel. Its authority is merely the authority of a witness, not of a judge; or an expert, not of a despot. We would carry the rejection of the Pope onward to the rejection of his two assessors, the Priest and the Emperor. We would sweep from the headship of the Church both the priest and the State. We are evangelical; we find Christianity not in the Church but in the Gospel. We are Churchmen; and we find in the Gospel alone the true charter and freedom of the Church. We are evangelical Free Churchmen. If we follow the Reformers by going to the Bible before the Church, we have no room for the priest because the New Testament has none. And if we go to the Gospel even before the Bible, we have also no room for the priest because the whole spiritual world is preoccupied and filled by the sole priesthood of Christ. If we go to the Gospel, which is the grand Reformation principle, we go to that which created both Church and Bible, and we have the secret of both. We live by faith in the grace of the cross and not of the mass. And we interpret all sacraments and give them their place by the Sacrament of the Word.

The real nature of the struggle to-day is a battle for the New Testament quality of English Christianity. What has to be done is to save the Church *from* the Church *for* the Bible and so for Christ. The Church has to be saved from its medieval self and from its patristic self for its New Testament self. We perpetuate the Reformation as the grand and crucial movement by which Christianity was saved *for religion;* and saved from mere culture, which is pagan, and from the priest, who is a Jew in soul. I do not say that that is a work left solely to us. That would be impertinent. It is partly ours because we are part of the Church and cannot see any section of it hampered with indifference, or being released without sympathy. It is partly ours also because the Parliament which at present controls the Established Church is as much ours as theirs. In so far as we are represented in Parliament we are masters of the ecclesiastical situation and responsible for it. But it is a work, it is a struggle, that is going on within the Established Church itself. So long as the finality of Scripture is held and fairly applied to the situation we need not fear the issue. And there are whole schools in the Established Church, like the great Cambridge school of New Testament scholarship, determined that the historic and scientific interpretation of Scripture shall be carried through at any cost to ecclesiastical tradition, seeing that the Bible has more to say to the Church than the Church to the Bible, and that the Bible can explain the Church as the Church can never explain the Bible.

WHERE DO WE REALLY GO WHEN WE GO BEHIND THE REFORMATION?

II

WHERE DO WE REALLY GO WHEN WE GO BEHIND THE REFORMATION?

WE are invited by the Catholic party in the Anglican Church now to abate our arid ardours about the Reformation, to leave the dreary negations of Protestantism, to abandon its hard, inhuman, and immoral theology, to turn from its dogmatic contentions and sterilities, to escape from its bare, cold, and irreverent ritual, to treat it as a movement that has long ago done its work, if ever it had any work to do worth the convulsion it caused ; and we are bidden to go behind it for our new point of departure, and to start afresh from the beautiful and glorious, true and tender medieval Church, with certain modern adaptations and new social sympathies. A reformed Catholicism is what the time needs and the Spirit prescribes to the Churches, a mere reformation on the lines of Trent, a readjustment of the Church, and not a regeneration of the Church's soul, or a fundamental change in the religious idea, or in the nature of Christianity, and so of faith. Catholicism and Christianity, we are told, are identical; and Catholicism is the true principle of progress.

I venture to accept the invitation so far as to examine that identity. I will go behind the Reformation. I will go to Catholicism. I will ask about its history and especially its origin, and with the best help that recent scholarship can afford us, I will inquire whether it is identical, or even coeval, with Christianity; and I hope to point out that it is neither identical nor cognate with Christianity, that it is due to an intrusion upon Christianity of the world, of the natural man and pagan culture. I hope to show that if we go behind the Reformation we cannot stop till we are landed inside the first century, inside the New Testament, inside the Gospels and the Epistles, inside the Cross, as St. Paul understood it, and faith as its direct and priestless answer. I think the greatest of all commentaries on the Gospels is the Epistles, that St. Peter and St. Paul are the interpreters, as they were the instructors, of Mark and Luke, and that the disposition to take the Gospels without the Epistles is one of those many tendencies in Protestantism which are in their genius Catholic, and make for Catholicism, and prepare for it in the public mind a congenial soil. There is a spiritual connection, subtle but powerful, between the Catholic movement and the movement which isolates the Gospels in the New Testament, and detaches their Christ from the Christ of Paul. The Church will be Catholic or Evangelical according as we dismiss Paul from his primacy among the apostles or keep him there. It is a conflict not between Paul and Peter, but between the New Testament Paul and Peter on the one side, and the ecclesiastical Peter on the other. If we go behind the Reformation, there is no stopping till we stop in Christ as interpreted by the faith of Paul.

The Reformation was not a new religion, but the rediscovery of the old. Therefore it did not break with the first like Christianity, but it went back on it, only farther back than Rome did. At the time of the Reformation there was a general consent, wherever its effect was owned at all, to go back upon the previous course of the Church, and seek its correction at some decisive era in the history of its past. There was a point, it was held, where the true course of the Spirit had been left, and the voice of the true Pilot had ceased to speak with commanding power. The Reformation Churches which remained Episcopal (especially the English) rejected the line of the popes, and took the older, higher line of the councils. Going back along this line, the English Church in the main fixed on the first six councils of the Church, covering the age of the fathers, the first four centuries. It found the authority for all the subsequent Church to lie with these councils, their canons and creeds, and with the Bible. But the continental Reformers went farther back—they went back to the first century, and to the New Testament alone. As Paul overleaped the later centuries of historic Judaism which had created the institutional part of the Old Testament, and went back to its origins in faithful Abraham and in God's promise there, so Luther passed over fifteen centuries of Catholicism, and took his stand upon Paul, and on the cross of Christ as it was interpreted by Paul to the direct and living faith of the sinful, grateful soul redeemed. The Christianity of the Reformation is the real Church of antiquity.

But to-day, while this process has been continued, there have been two great changes introduced into it, and it is the renewed study of the Bible, the Protestant treatment of it, that has caused both. It has been found, first, that the New Testament itself embodies various points of view; it is not absolutely homogeneous in respect of doctrine, and it carries in it some views which were more true for the circumstances of the first century than for those of the nineteenth. So the Protestant movement has been forced down upon a small section even of the first century for its object and standard of faith—upon the few years covering the life, and especially the public life, and work of Christ. " Back to Christ" has been the cry. And we cannot stop there. We have not a biography of Christ in the modern sense to admit us to the very centre of His character and motive. And Christ shared on some points the views of His contemporaries; without prejudice to His saving work, He may be held to have claimed no final authority on matters of scientific knowledge—say, of the origin of the Old Testament, or the causes of disease. Consequently within Christ Himself the final authority is located less in His teaching than in His person and work—especially His work on the cross. From the Gospel *about* Christ we penetrate to Christ as the Gospel, as the grace of God in action, as the living grace of God, the acting, dying, rising, redeeming, reconciling, effectual, conquering grace of God. The standard and authority is the Gospel in Christ—the cross. And from the first century our classic and commanding time is narrowed down almost to a point, but an infinite point—like a man in the universe—and all is staked and focussed on the cross. The Gospel takes the place as our standard which used to be taken by the Bible. That is the change for Protestantism; the authority of the Gospel is the standard of authority for the Bible. We do not ask if a truth is in the Bible, but in the Gospel, in Christ's person and work.

But there is another change which here concerns us more. It presses upon those who canonise, not the New Testament, but the first four centuries of the Church. It is caused by the discovery that the difference between the Church even of the second century and that of the first is an immense one, and one which grows as scientific and impartial research goes on. At the end of the apostolic age the history of the Church, it has been said, enters a tunnel for about a generation. We have almost no data for it. And when it comes out the Church has undergone a change whose tremendous importance is even now the largest influence on the Church in the world. It has begun to be the CATHOLIC Church, and it has ceased in some essential points to be the Church of the New Testament. The train has crossed some frontier, and the guards, drivers, uniforms, even engines, are changed. That which was destroyed by the Reformation was this Catholicism by which the second century swamped the first. It was not a system which had broken away from the first four centuries, but one which broke away from the first century, from the New Testament. There are two senses of the word Church in the New Testament, either the Church local or the Church ideal. The third sense, of the Catholic Church, the huge religious state, is not in the New Testament at all. That is to say, that conception of the Church on which they stand who unchurch the Free Churches does not exist in the New Testament. It is not earlier than the second century. It is Catholicism. *It was Catholicism that the Reformation broke.* Catholicism was the perversion which settled down on the Church in the second century and identified itself with the first. Many of us have been taught to regard the Church's first great apostasy from the New Testament ideal as connected with Constantine and his patronage or Christianity as the State religion about 320 A.D. But we must go farther back to seek the real apostasy, the deflection of faith, which prepared the Church for succumbing to the patronage of the empire. It was in the second century, when the Church became mastered by the imperial idea, when it aspired to be one universal Church, a grand hierarchy, a spiritual *imperium in imperio*. It was then that the Catholic Church arose, as distinct from the Church of the New Testament. In the New Testament Church the unity was wholly unseen, and its invisible reality acted through a visible multitude of independent communities.

Catholicism, then, be it clearly understood, arose in the second century, and it was historically bound to arise, I admit. It arose out of historic necessities, which we can partly but poorly trace. The chief of these necessities was the rise of Gnosticism, of which we see the first beginnings in the Epistle to the Colossians and the Epistles of John. This was the Christian rationalism of the first Church. But it was a mystical rationalism, with great spiritual pretensions. It was like the theosophies we hear of in our own time. It was a vague combination of mystical vision with the speculative science of the day. With masses of people it was very plausible. The popular Christian mind of that day was as ignorant and gullible as west-end women are with " Christian science "; and the movement threatened to run away with the whole of Christianity. If it had, Christianity would, humanly speaking, have been as surely destroyed as it would have been earlier if Paul had not risen to save it from Judaism. So now it had to be saved from paganism in this insidious form. How? By organization. That was the power which an imperial age best understood. The salvation was effected by organizing the Church into a rigid unity, with the bishops at its head. You might call this in a way a Reformation. It saved the Church from a pagan corruption, as Luther's did. But its means were very different. This first Reformation was by the bishop, the second was by the Gospel. The first was by machinery, the second was by faith. The Catholic Church is machine-made, the Evangelical is soul-made, made by faith. The Catholic Church is a work of skill, the Evangelical is a work of genius. The Church was saved from the Gnostics by becoming an institution; it was saved a millennium and a half later from the Catholics by becoming an inspiration.

In this episcopal reformation of the second century the old congregational system of the New Testament was left behind. The public need forced the local Churches first into great provincial Churches with a bishop, and these again into a great universal or Catholic Church, with a bishop of bishops at the head of all. Episcopacy began what the papacy completed. I noticed in the Pan-Anglican Synod of a year or two ago a proposal (which was not allowed to go very far) that the Archbishop of Canterbury should be invested with a certain primacy over all the bishops of the Episcopal Church in England or in America. This was, of course, resisted by the American bishops. But it was an exact repetition of what took place in the beginning of the papacy in the third century. It was English imperialism trying to force itself on the Church, just as Roman imperialism did in its time. And the same appetite for rule would force itself upon us of the Free Churches but for the men of controversy and vigilance.

Now I would repeat that Catholicism, with the

supremacy of the monarchical bishop, may have been a historical necessity, and may have saved the Church at a great crisis. Organization has that use to a certain degree. There are junctures that call for centralization and even for a dictator. But the peril is that the dictator may stay on as emperor, that the protector may prolong himself into a dynasty, that the ally invited in to repel an enemy may remain as a conqueror. And this is what happened with the bishop. He soon became not only useful, but indispensable, permanent. He developed a theory of himself. He discovered that he was involved in the absolute and eternal constitution of the Church. He found, and declared, that there could be no Church and no salvation without a bishop. The Church as organized became canonized. It was no longer true that Christ was where two or three were gathered in His name, but only where there was a legitimate bishop. Where the bishop was, and there alone, was a Church.

There is a remarkable parallel to all this in Old Testament history. Israel, in its most spiritual time, was captured by a Catholicism of centralization, to which in the end it succumbed. No sooner had prophetism taken its noblest and holiest form in Jeremiah than it was seized by a close religion of the priest and temple. The Judaism which took the place of the old prophetic Hebraism, and grew into the damning righteousness of scribe and Pharisee, arose in the priestly centralization of all worship at Jerusalem, which won the assent even of the prophets of the time. This was a measure which took effect in connection with the discovery of the book of Deuteronomy in the temple in the reign of King Josiah, about 620 B.C. It was, perhaps, a necessary step in the circumstances. The local shrines of Jehovah, in the midst of a rude and half-pagan population, were scenes of abuse which threatened to swamp in heathen syncretism the purer faith. But it was a policy of emergency which, through the anarchy of the exile shortly after, became normal and perpetual, like a war-tax which lives on as the main element in a peace revenue, or like a president or consul who comes out of a convulsion an emperor. It was a step with the gravest consequences. It developed into a policy in which the free, prophetic, nonconformist spirit died, and all life came to be organized by a hierarchy into the most minute and terrible ritual of conduct ever seen. It was the beginning of the policy which turned the State into a Church, and into a Church which committed the crime of the world. That was Hebrew Catholicism, the sacerdotalised community of Israel. And that is what Christian Catholicism would do if it had its way, and did do so far as it had. Many of its advocates say it would not, and they are honest enough. But there is a spiritual logic which over-rules individual ideas in such matters. And the end I indicate is the irresistible conclusion to which Catholic principles work out on the field of history. Hebrew Catholicism, in spite of many profound ideas and symbols, yet killed the religion of Israel, and made a new religion necessary. Christianity was a new religion, and not a development of the old. It was the child of the old, and not its manhood. And what that terrible Judaism was to the spirit of prophecy Catholicism is to Christianity. And the Reformation was not a new religion only because it was the rediscovery of the old, the earliest Christianity, which Catholicism so early as the second century had lost.

And there is this further analogy. The law books born in the Judaic age, like Leviticus, carried back the whole organization of the worship to the time of Moses, and were themselves believed to belong to that time and that author. The new cultus imported itself into the original institution of the religion, and identified itself with it. It was in like fashion that episcopacy and the priesthood, through mere historic growths, referred themselves very early to the original foundation of Christ. They imported into New Testament words which had no such meaning the monarchical bishop, the apostolic succession, and the priestly prerogative of sacrifice and absolution. It is not strange that the Catholic system should make great use of the Old Testament for the Christian Church. And it was only working the same vein in a richer lode in its employment of the spurious Ignatian letters and the forged donation of Constantine.

This tremendous change from Scriptural to Catholic Christianity took place with amazing rapidity. We are surprised. But we must not forget two things. First, the age. It was an age when the Roman, organized, imperial idea of society was uncontested. Our modern democratic ideas did not as yet exist. The monarch stood for the multitude. Peoples followed the religion of their rulers. There was no communal right. The people, in our modern sense, did not exist. But, it is said, there was the model of the first Churches, the New Testament Churches, which have made our modern Free Churches. Yes, but that suggests the next fact which must not be forgotten. The memory of the first century was preserved chiefly in the unwritten tradition of those very officers whose position was to be enhanced. The New Testament had then hardly an existence. Its various books were there among others, and were read, but they were not authoritative; there was no canon. That selection was not yet made. The canon and place of Scripture was one of the great gifts, probably the greatest gift, of Catholicism to the future. But as yet the canon was not there to keep Catholicism in its place. It was put there by Catholicism for its own support, as one of the greatest engines with which to fight the Gnostic heresy, and set up a standard against its speculative extravagance.

Catholicism with the bishop, then, arose to meet a historic need. It was created not by divine fiat, but by a historic necessity. It is not there with an absolute and sole divine right, as unique as Christ or the Church. But having come into existence, it went on to ascribe itself to divine fiat. It traced itself to the Apostles. It claimed to carry down what could not be carried down—the unique privilege of Apostles who had seen the Lord. It gave itself an absolute right in the Church, instead of a relative and historic. It was good for the situation, but it became megalomaniac and said it was essential for ever. And in the comparative absence of a canon of scripture, it had little difficulty in making this claim good. I cannot stop to trace this process, but it can be traced. It persuaded the whole Church that without it there was no Church, therefore no salvation. To reject the bishop was to reject Christ and court perdition. The great apostle of this false gospel was Cyprian, in the third century, who was for the early Church what

Laud was for the Anglican. Laud, indeed, is called by his biographer, Heylin, *Cyprianus Anglicanus*.

Now let it be well understood that there *is* this huge gulf between the Church of the second century and that of the first. It is a truth which never was so clearly realised till the critical scholarship of this century dealt with the records both in and out of the Bible. It is a truth that is bound to make its way in a learned Church. It is making its way, and it is having its effect. It is an immense help to every contention of ours; for it carries our principles home, with all the weight of ecclesiastical and historic science, to circles that could not be expected to have anything to do with a Congregational Union, or a Liberation Society, or even a Protestant Alliance.

What received its death-blow at the Reformation was not simply the papacy, but Catholicism. We do not need to regard even Roman Episcopacy as antichrist. We need only regard it as having become an anachronism. Episcopacy may have been historically necessary, as in circumstances it may be preferable to-day. It does not become Catholicism till it claim to be sole. Catholicism is monopolist Episcopacy. It is an old historic necessity, which has forgotten its place and outstayed its time. It was a guest of the Church with no more taste than to linger on when the household groaned under its presence. It was welcome when it came, and it might have been willingly retained in a permanent position in the household of faith, if it had not taken control of the establishment, and forbidden the other branches of the family to cross the door. What the Reformation did was not even to turn Catholicism out of the house, but to teach it its place in the house as one of many, and certainly not the firstborn. And the Reformation did this by restoring the original New Testament idea of faith, by restoring faith to its creative place in the *government* of the Church. It was the first time that the New Testament had been seriously and directly dealt with since it had become the canon. It was the first time it had assumed its true power and place. Up till then it had been entirely in the hands of the Catholicism that constructed the canon for its own purpose, and therefore interpreted it in its own sense. Now the Spirit, the gospel, took the New Testament out of the hands of the Church as an institution, and gave it into the hands of faith. It took the New Testament, covered with dust, out of the bishop's chancellory and the priest's breviary, and laid it open on the believer's table.

I say the Reformation put an end to Catholicism by restoring the New Testament idea of faith. It not only took us back from the fathers of the first four centuries to the first century, but it forced us to recognise that *the change from the first century to the second was more than a change in the Church's constitution. It was a change in the Church's FAITH*—which is a much more serious thing. The Church, in entering the social conflict of the early centuries, had lost the purity of its first idea. It became wide and popular, but at the cost of its truth and purity. It conquered the world by becoming more or less worldly. It gained the world, but it lost in its own soul. It became an empire, but it ceased, in proportion, to be a communion. Becoming Catholic, it ceased, in a measure, to be holy and apostolic. It was secularised in the effort to capture the age for Christ. It was seduced by the world it set out to reclaim. It won power, but it lost in faith. A change destined to be fatal passed over its idea of faith, which became sacramental, priestly, episcopal, institutional, instead of ethical, spiritual, and evangelical. The gospel became a new law; and virtue became a thing of order, instead of a thing of the new conscience.

That is why I say that the present struggle is a struggle for the purity and permanence of Christian faith. It is not for reverence, or for Christian piety, or for Christian philanthropy; these exist as richly among Catholics, especially Anglo-Catholics, as among ourselves. But it is for the true, original, and permanent nature of Christian faith, for faith's future, for the future of Christianity. For a religion is just as its faith; and Christianity can only be the religion of the future if it retain the original idea of faith as its motive power and working capital. Our breach with the absolute and sacerdotal Episcopalians is not one which it can do any good to gloze over and fine down to a mere verbal or historic affair. The conflict will be much clearer, shorter, and more fruitful if we let the issue be as distinct as we can make it. And it is by way of doing so that I say, with all who are disposed to be thorough in this matter, that the change from the Christian brotherhoods and communities of the first century to the Christian Church of the second was one not merely of order, but of faith. The difference between the Free Churches and the Catholics, Anglican or Roman, is one of faith, and not of Church order merely. It is more religious than ecclesiastical. And whoever passes from the one to the other does not simply adopt another Church polity, but another, and in one case a less Christian, form of faith, another gospel, as Paul said in a similar juncture, which indeed is not another, because in the strict sense it is not a gospel. It is a return of mere law, in which distinctive gospel is practically lost.

Is it not clear that it must be so? The mystery and the power of Christianity is faith—understood not merely as a religious sympathy or affection, but as direct, personal communion with Christ, based on forgiveness of sins direct from Him to the conscience. It is not bound up absolutely with any external ordinances or institutions. These are but functional to faith, not organic; historic, but not essential or eternal. Believe in the Lord Jesus Christ, and thou shalt be saved—not in the Church, not in the sacraments, not in the priesthood. All these have their great worth as exhibitions and energies of the Church, not as conditions between Christ and the Lord. They are not objects of faith. But, in the change which made Catholicism, this communion with Christ is made to depend absolutely on external forms and conditions. That is the essence of Catholicism in one word. *It is fixed and consecrated institutionalism, whether episcopal or sacerdotal.* That is a more deep and serious perversion of the Church than its connection with the State. One of the chief reasons why it is wished to set the Church free from the State is this—that the Church of all faithful men may be more free to deal with that Catholic corruption which only Christian freedom can deal with, only Christian directness, originality, and vitality of evangelical faith. When the Church is free from the political institution, it will still have to deal with the clerical institution. Because, when a Church is in the first place institutional, it is only in the second place evangelical; and a

Church is in the first place institutional which refuses an equal recognition to any Church which is equally evangelical. The Church of England is to-day more of an institution than of a gospel. It idolises an order and an office, at the cost of Christian truth, faith, and love. "By taste are ye saved." The Church of an evangelical faith will have to deal with that idolatry. Faith will have to make the Church sit much more loosely to each form of polity, and especially to destroy the historic fallacy and delusion that episcopacy is original or essential to a true Church and a true faith. Such a belief is fatal to Christian faith at last. It is a departure which touches the very marrow and nature of faith as due to the person and work of Christ alone. I urge you anew to be very clear as to what the real nature of Catholicism is, and its incompatibility with the faith of the New Testament, and especially of Paul. Do not waste on the Pope, who is a remote danger for us, the breath that should be used to cool or extinguish the Catholic claim, which is our near foe. The enemy is not an institution, but a spirit — institutionalism. Catholicism—let it be clear—is not the USE of an institutional Church. For then the Presbyterian would fall under the ban, the Methodist, and indeed every single church of our own order which is well and permanently organized. Catholicism is the idolatry of a particular form of institution, and its monopoly for salvation. It is making it an object of faith. If any man says, as the second century did say, that membership of an outward organization represented by bishops (or we might say presbyters if they made the claim) is essential to a man's being a Christian; if he identify that episcopal organization, from Christ's institution downwards, with the Kingdom of God; if he thus rest the Church upon an office or an order, instead of the office on the Church—then our difference with him is not a difference of opinion, but a difference of faith. He has damaged the Christian faith. He has thrust between the soul and Christ an institution which neither Christ nor His gospel puts there. He has become a member of the Church, more than a member of Christ. If a man say that only the bishop and his nominees are the teachers and guides appointed *by God* for His Church; that there is no Church where there is no bishop; that only subordination to the bishop gives communion with Christ in any regular way; that the rest may see their Saviour occasionally, but cannot have the indwelling spirit—if he say that, is it not clear that between him and us there is a great gulf fixed by faith itself? And we can never rest—the Holy Spirit forbids us to rest—till that perverted faith is restored to the living way. This battle is going to end in a great clearing and uplifting of faith for all the Churches. We have to insist that this

Catholic perversion is choking the Gospel with a specious form of the law which the Gospel came to set us free from. I do not say the Gospel destroyed law, or institutions which are in the name of law and order. The Gospel did not come to rid us of law, but to give us freedom in connection with it, to make it our servant when it had been our master. And so it enables us to use Church institutions and keep them in their place. But this institutionalism, which makes an official or an office part of the Gospel, is simply bringing in at the window the reign of law which St. Paul, in Christ's name, turned out at the door. It is restoring to the temple the business which Christ whipped out. It is destroying what made faith a real gospel and release. It is surrendering the principle of redemption. I speak of the system. I do not say it so appears to those who hold it. But I must say that the Gospel is in principle given up to the world where the Catholic claim is made for either bishop or priest, or both. Priest and bishop ! We cannot fail to see that scientific history would enable us to deal far more easily with the episcopal monopoly of the Church if the bishop had not become merged in the priest. The trouble to-day is that the bishops who rule the Church are too much priests ; and they are said by some within the Episcopal Church itself to appoint to the training colleges of the clergy heads more sacerdotal than themselves, and more narrow because more academic, more secluded from public life and criticism. It is the priestly and not the administrative functions of the bishop that explain the tenacity of Episcopacy. It is his relation to the sacraments that is the point of conflict more than his relation to polity. I have no objection to Episcopacy as a good polity among others equally good. In the *Contemporary Review* for last August (1898) you may read the scientific evidence for what I have been saying about the post-apostolic origin of the episcopate. It is an article written conjointly by two of the soundest scholars—one of them an Oxford clergyman, and one a tutor of Mansfield College. It is hard to think that there would be a resistance to such scientific proof were the question not confused by prepossessions about sacerdotal grace which make it a religious instead of a historical question. Very early—in the third century—the two streams met and fused, the episcopal and the sacerdotal. The priest and the bishop were rolled into one. The process can be traced. The presiding presbyter became the sole minister of each Church. Then the Church came to rest on the bishop, instead of the bishop on the Church. The bishop was supposed to stand exactly in the place of an apostle, and the Church was said to rest on the foundation of the apostles. (They forgot the addition of "prophets"—

the preachers who stood alongside of the apostles in the first Church.) In virtue of this succession the bishop possessed an infallibility in Christian truth which was miraculously transmitted in his appointment. Moreover, as a matter of order, no sacraments were valid or effectual unless administered by the bishop of the Church or by his agents. Meanwhile, mystical and even magical value was ascribed to the sacraments and to those who dispensed them. The bishop not only stood for the Church, but for Christ in His sacrificial power. The infallibility of the bishop was augmented by the miraculous gift of the priest, and the same person stood for both.

In Anglican Catholicism the infallibility of the bishop has virtually been dropped. I doubt if there are many who would now stand even for the doctrinal infallibility of the bishops of the first four centuries. They are regarded (as Canon Gore says) as "focussing" rather than creating the faith of the Church. The line of episcopal infallibility was retained only in the Roman branch of Catholicism, and it found its logical conclusion in the Vatican dogma of the Pope's infallibility in 1870. But the *sacerdotal* miracle in the bishop as chief cleric has been retained by the Anglican Church, and is to-day the real nerve of the episcopal prerogative in those who take it most religiously. The Englishman cares less for truth than for action. So he could dispense with a bishop who had the gift of miraculous truth, but he kept a bishop who had the power of miraculous action. The apostolic legacy was not for him the power of preaching Gospel truth so as to rouse faith, but the power of doing priestly acts so as to mediate God. The ministry becomes not an office for the sake of order, but it becomes an order and a sacrament.

It is this false apostolicity that we have to resist, and we have to resist it on the great reformation principle, which was twofold—a subjective appeal to Christian experience of sin and its forgiveness, and an objective appeal to the Church of the first century as represented by the New Testament. We can win this battle only by a revival of faith, by more religion and more Bible. I do not think we can fight this battle, as we are sometimes told to do, by going out to the public and doing more good than our opponents. Doing good is only understood by the public in the sense of philanthropy, and not in the evangelical, spiritual sense which alone tells in this issue. If it is a question of practising more philanthropy than our adversaries, we Congregationalists at least may give up the battle. We have not the organization, the wealth, the devotees. No minister with his voluntary staff can cope in this respect with the priest and his staff of curates ("My curate is an admirable man. He is running about the parish the whole day ") and the leisured men and women to whom their creed and Church is a ruling and ascetic passion. But no Church question should really be settled by an appeal to philanthropy, or to the public. It is a piece of cant to say, as the man in the street does, that the priest cannot be very dangerous, because he is a man of such unselfish devotion, and does so much good among the poor. Men often admire the devotedness of others because it saves themselves trouble. Devotedness is not the test of truth, or else the Jesuits would be the true clergy. Nor is philanthropy the test, else the apostolic succession must run through St. Francis, St. Vincent, Howard, Fry, Müller, and Shaftesbury. But the main point is that the priest himself, to do him justice, would never consent to rest his case upon the zeal or philanthropy of devoted priests. He unites with us in taking much higher ground. He appeals to the Divine order, the Divine will, the Divine commission, the nature of Christian religion. And, like us, he does not make his appeal to the public, but to the faithful—the really religious, to those who care for the will of God, and can be made to own it. He chafes under his parliamentary Church. He demands that the Church rule the Church, that Christ be master in His own house. That is the principle whose defence has cost ourselves so much for so long. He objects to have the unbeliever settling Church affairs like belief, worship, ministry. It is that principle of the Free Churches that is working Disestablishment from within. Let us never cease preaching the principle. Let us welcome it whether it be preached by priests, friars, or liberationists. They are all liberationists when it comes to that. They believe in the Church's spiritual freedom. And they perceive it can only come by Disestablishment. Set even the priest free from the control of the State, and from its social support; free to be dealt with by the Gospel, by the believer. If he is to be taught his place it must be by spiritual men and means. A spirit mightier than his own must eject him. It is not to the public, the voter, that we must look for the victory of our cause, but to the believer, to those who care for the will and word of God, to the men of faith, to those who seek the principle of this matter in the true nature of the Church, and find the true nature of the Church within the Bible, in the Gospel. If our cause be weak it is so because we are reading everything but the Bible. One of the preacher's great difficulties is in dealing with people who are checking him not by their Bibles, but by their feelings, or their personal preferences. But the reading of the Bible is not enough. It is the study of the Bible that we fail in. And it is that failure that leaves us so exposed to the ecclesiastical perversions and plausibilities of the hour. Is there that deep gulf between the Catholicism which had captured the Church in the second century, and the Christian brotherhood of faith and love which was the Church of the first century? You must go to your New Testament and see. You resent the priest in the name of your individual freedom. That is not enough. Do you do it in the name of a universal priesthood, which has sunk your individual freedom in obedience to the sacrifice of Christ? That is the point. You resist to the utmost the confessional and the intrusion of the priest into your family, between you and your children, you and your wife. Yes; but why do you so resent it? Is it simply as a sturdy, honest, British home-lover? or is it as a man who chiefly obeys the Christian principle, both of marriage and of the ministry? Because if the New Testament, if the Gospel of Christ, said that the priest had a Divine right in the bosom of your family, there is no other right strong enough to bar him out. Certainly the burly Briton with his house as his castle could not. You admit the minister to perform your marriage. Why? Why do you suffer the Church to step in and say that you shall not follow the impulse of your mutual and private affections without her consent and blessing? Because you believe that marriage is a Christian institution. And the ground of that is with Christ in the New Testament. It is not in rules or canons of the Church. So, in the same way, if the New Testament said or implied that the priest had a right in Christ's name to set up his confessional between you and your wife, no *natural* resistance of yours would have any right. A spiritual right takes precedence of a natural. It would mean no more than the mere recalcitrance of those poor defiant egoists—male and female—who say that neither Church nor State has any right to meddle with their private affections, and who, therefore, live together without the seal of either. But how do you know that the minister of Christ has not this right? It can only be from a knowledge of the New Testament. It is your duty to be certain that that conception of Christ's minister is not there. It is your Christian duty, before you take any extreme line on a Christian issue, to know what the mind of Christ on the subject is. And the only source of your knowledge about it is in the New Testament. That is faith's court of appeal. I do not say the New Testament is faith's statute book, because the New Testament is not statutory. It is the court of the King's bench, the seat of a living Lord and Judge, and the source of a Holy Spirit who guides us, by personal contact and practice and experience, into all truth. He does not so much give us our decisions, but He gives us power, light, and guidance to make our decisions. But there must be personal contact, personal experience, personal faith.

I lay incessant stress on that word faith—personal faith. The message of the Church to the world is not to bid men love, but to bid them believe. The message has come, in the refinement of our religious culture, to be too much, and too expressly, a call for love. That is not the true evangelical note. It is the Catholic note—the note of the Roman saint, the monastic community; the note of socialist piety rather than of the Church's faith. It is not the Reformation note, nor is it a true development of the Reformation note. Do not preach the duty of love, but the duty of faith. Do not begin by telling men in God's name that they should love one another. That is no more than an amiable Gospel. And it is an impossible Gospel till faith give the power to love. They cannot do it. Tell them how God has loved them. Bid them as sinners trust that. Preach faith as the direct answer to God's love. The first answer to the love of God is not love, but faith. Preach faith and the love will grow out of it of itself. Loving, *as a Gospel*, is Catholic. The Protestant and evangelical Gospel is believing. Believe in Christ crucified and the love will come. Love must come if we believe in love. But it has first to be believed in before it is imitated. "We

WHAT IS BEHIND THE REFORMATION? 105

are not saved by the love we feel, but by the love we trust." And what we need in our preaching to-day is not so much Reformation truths, nor even Reformation enthusiasm, but the Reformation *note* and order of faith—of faith as an evangelical, personal experience, faith as the peace and confidence of being redeemed and forgiven by the death of Christ and by nothing else whatever.

We are to-day in a similar position to that which the Church had to face in the second century—similar, yet with one essential difference. We are faced by a nineteenth-century gnosis of science fused with imagination, a gnosis of savant, socialist, and poet. We are confronted by a modern rationalism, culture, humanism, mysticism, half Christian, half pagan, which takes the Christian truths and terms and trims them down, under plea of filling them out, to its own sympathies, ideas, aspirations, principles, and morals. The peril of this is felt by the Church, the true Church, in all branches of it. And various means are taken to avert the danger. The means taken by the second century was organization. It was to close up the ranks of the Church, to draw the independent Churches together, not into a federation, but into a huge spiritual bureaucracy, to increase the episcopate, and put more power into the hands of the bishops. They were placed in a new and unique relation to the apostles. And they were fortified by the addition of a priestly power quite different from the doctrinal infallibility which the apostolic connection was supposed to give. Now that is exactly what the ruling movement in the Anglican Church to-day is doing. They are fighting a real and present peril with only the means most ready to hand in the second century. What they do not duly recognise is that history does not repeat itself in this simple way. The very work of Catholicism itself has essentially changed the situation. Catholicism has utterly changed the situation, for one thing, by giving us the canon of Scripture, and through that the Reformation. The canon did not exist in the second century. There was nothing objective to fall back on except the tradition of the apostles' teaching, surviving in the Churches they had founded, and re-echoed by the leaders, bishops, and teachers of these Churches. It was the state of things which Wesleyanism would have shown if its Churches to-day had only had the early Methodists, the associates of Wesley, to appeal to, instead of his writings (to say nothing of the Bible). No Church can exist without an objective authority. And the only objective authority possible in the second century was the bishops, as representing what was believed to be the apostolic tradition. They were unsatisfactory representatives, but they were all that there was. And they did give us a real successor to the original apostolate, which superseded themselves. It was the New Testament. *The real successor of the apostles is the New Testament.* That is now freely in the hands of the Church. It is an objective which stands while the Church may waver with the floods and gales of the time, or falter with the weight of work or years. Our modern situation is entirely changed by the possession of the New Testament, and by an understanding of it far truer, deeper, richer than that possessed even by the second century. Now, what one misses in the Anglican movement is a due recognition of this fact. I say a *due* recognition, for it is not without some recognition. And by a due recognition I mean an appeal to the Church to go back solely upon personal acquaintance with the New Testament, as earnest as the appeal on behalf of priest or bishop. Catholicism had really done its work when it gave to the Church the New Testament. The great gift of Catholicism to the Church was the power to overcome Catholicism by the Scriptures. It ought then to have got slowly out of the way, had it not been captured and prisoned by imperial and priestly ideas. As it was, it was destroyed in principle as soon as the Bible came to its own in the Reformation, and living faith fell at the feet of living grace. A great institutional Church may be a doubtful gift to the world. It is anything but a real gift when it claims a monopoly and an idolatry due only to an essential part of the Gospel. But there is no doubt about the gift that the Catholic Church gave the world in the Bible. And the greatness of that gift lies in the Bible's power to make us forget the donor in the author, the Church in the Redeemer. We are grateful to the Church till we discover that its gift is meant as a Trojan horse, as an engine for our conquest. The Bible is not there to enhance the Church, but both Bible and Church are there to enhance the Gospel. The Bible has more to do for the Church than ever the Church has done or can do for the Bible. And the Bible never does so much for the Church as it does when it puts us in a position to judge, condemn, and reform the whole Church by its light. It is only that light that can reform the Church. It is not the light of nature, the common man, the worldly parliament. Set the Church free from these things, to be acted on by its own Bible. Deliver the Church from the voter for the believer. What the clergy say is, deliver it from the citizen for the priest. What the Erastians say is, deliver it from the priest for the citizen. What the Free Churches say is, deliver it from the citizen for the believer, and let Christ come to His own in the living faith of His own.

If we go behind the Reformation, therefore, it is

not in the medieval Church that we can stop, nor in the Church of the fathers and the first four centuries or the first six councils; nor can we stop with the second century and its bishops, nor even with the end of the first. We are carried on by the Holy Ghost to the source of His own action upon the world, to the person of Christ, to His work on the cross, to direct contact with the Gospel of that grace and the sacrifice of that one Priest. So being justified by faith, we have peace with God through Jesus Christ, and confidence unto the end.

WHAT DID LUTHER REALLY DO?

III

WHAT DID LUTHER REALLY DO?

I

IF we ask what the real nature of the issue is in a serious crisis of the Church we must always fall back on its conception of faith. The contention implies on one side or the other some serious decay and involves some serious reform there. If there be in the Church long *malaise*, resulting in acute periodic disturbance, we may be sure that the seat of the mischief is in some vital part; and in the severest forms of it, it is in the vital centre; and the vital centre of the Church is faith. What is then needed is not a revival, and it is not primarily a reformation, far less is it mere regulation Acts.

The present crisis is far too serious to be dealt with by parliamentary regulation. It is even beyond the reach of episcopal reformation. The priest has broken loose from the bishop. He claims an authority above the bishop; he goes behind him, as, in a sense, we do. He appeals to some authority prior to the bishop, which made the bishop, and which the bishop must obey. He goes to the Church, as, in another sense, we do. He accuses the bishop, for the sake of the State connection, of betraying the Church and the Catholic faith. For him the Church is virtually the priesthood. There, of course, we are not with him; but we can only welcome his appeal to the Church from the episcopate because our own appeal is to the Church, and our inquiry is, what makes it? We hold that the Church is made by the Gospel and its Word of Life held forth to the world. Catholicism holds that it is made by something institutional, by the twofold institution of the bishop and the priest. But priest and bishop are now in antagonism. And we cannot but be glad that the institutional idea of the Church is thus proving unworkable as its essential idea. It all tends to place the Church on its one sound base of a living, personal, evangelical faith.

We come back always to that. Every crisis drives us in upon our *faith*. And in respect of faith what is needed is not a revival. We have had several revivals during the last century, but they are only forcing the greater crisis. They have not brought peace to the Church, or solidity of conviction, energy, and life. We have had the Evangelical revival, the Oxford High Church revival, and the Broad Church revival. And they have left us where we are to-day. What is it all moving to? What is it that the Spirit is striving with man, with the Church, to bring to pass? A new Act of Parliament, a new episcopal charge, the schism of an extreme priestly section from the Established Church? Do mountains labour of mice like these? What we need, what the Spirit moves to, is a regeneration of the central idea of faith, a return to the New Testament and the Reformation idea of it, a development of that idea which has been arrested both in Episcopacy and in Protestantism—in the one by politics, in the other by a debased orthodoxy, or by impatient social programmes.[1] What is going on is a war against Catholicism in both its Roman, its Anglican, and its Protestant form. The Church is struggling for its spiritual life with a Catholicism of order or of doctrine which took possession of it in the second century, which was destroyed in principle at the Reformation, but which in practice

[1] The laicising of religion in Protestantism had its own perils, and one of them was the secularising of it from which we now suffer. The world that faith was to leaven has captured and sterilised faith. What the State has done in one way society has done in another. This was a risk that Protestantism had to run like Christianity itself. The Reformation had one true note of faith in that it was a tremendous venture, the work of a courage superhuman, and either diabolic or divine. Happily hazard is not the badge of error, as security is not the sole effect of salvation. Nothing risks so much as faith, and there are few things more perilous than religion, especially to outward finality and peace.

holds it to this day. And the root of the quarrel is to be found in the conception of faith which distinguishes the Church of the New Testament, and of the Reformation, from that of Catholicism.

I would be particularly understood to mean that the strife is not confined to the Established Church. The strife there can really only be settled by a change which affects the whole religious mind of this country, and by a voice which recalls the Protestant and Nonconformist as well as the Catholic to the Gospel of Christ, from paths that are fatal at last. The war with Catholicism is acute in the Established Church, but it is waged also in the bosom of Nonconformist Protestantism itself. Even there faith has to suffer from other forms of the Catholic idea, from the theological relics of scholastic orthodoxy on the one side, and especially from culture on the other; from a Pelagian, synergistic humanism, or from a Franciscan piety whose idea is a compassionate philanthropy much more fine than final—as far from final as monasticism was for the regeneration of the Church. Assisi was well, but it did not do what had to be done, and what was done at Wittenberg, Worms, and the Wartburg.

The issue which is raised concerns the essential nature of Christianity. The war is for the expulsion of paganism by faith, or its reduction to a secondary or tertiary place; and by paganism is not meant the heathen cults, but the practical supremacy of the natural man and the supersession of revelation in the ideal of life and the soul. It is, therefore, clear that the war must be waged in Protestant communities themselves, to save them from the humanism and naturalism which are Catholic in their spirit and result. The great pagan of Protestantism—Goethe—was in spirit and tendency Catholic. All art, literature, and culture gravitate there when they become the ruling interest of life. And any reconstruction of Christianity upon these lines chiefly does more for a Catholic revival in the long run than it does for the New Testament faith of the Gospel. Our great danger is not Ultramontanism; it is a far subtler Romanism than that, and one which prepares the soil on which Ultramontanism finds ready growth. The enemy is Catholicism, the worship of system in society or creed. From this Protestantism is but partly purged. The Reformation was a reformation but in part, and that part was soon overtaken by a resurgence of the Catholic habit of mind in the shape of orthodoxy. The Protestant orthodoxy of last century was Catholic in its spirit. It was institutional, confessional. And no less Catholic is, on the one hand, the philosophic liberalism of to-day; and, on the other hand, our refined and literary mysticism. Hegelianism, with its love of system, if it remain positive, tends to the institutional and established

Churches; and the Friends who leave their Society and do not turn Unitarian gravitate to the æsthetic and sacerdotal Church.

II

To aid us in adjusting Faith to Humanism let us ask, what was the real work and permanent value of Luther, and in what sense does he keep his value for us to-day? I take Luther of course as the symbol and representative of the whole Reformation.

Luther is a most heroic figure, but it is not as a hero that he is of perennial value to the world. As a hero he would be merely an æsthetic object, a colossal representative of modern individualism facing the old and corporate order of things. As a hero he is a magnificent organ of human power and freedom, a glorious expression of human courage and human conscience. He enters into innumerable pictures and lessons upon human valour, stoutness of heart, and fidelity to conviction. Luther before the Diet at Worms, with his " Here I stand ; I can do no other. So help me God," is one of the stock legends of moral courage and the lone good fight.

But as such he is not solitary in history. He did nothing unique in its nature. We may be proud and thankful as men to think that there have been many men, in many ages, and in many causes, that have shown moral heroism of this kind. The present age does not breed them as freely as some, but they are not extinct even to-day. And we must recognise them even among those whose principles we have to resist. There was a grandeur in Charles V. as well as in Luther, a heroism of empire as well as a heroism of revolt. If you are to honour men for mere sincerity, or veracity, above all things, you will have a pantheon as mixed as worship of that kind made Carlyle's to be, whose heroes ranged from Luther the godly to the pagan Goethe and the godless Frederick. If you are to make fidelity to conscience the supreme standard, you must pay as much respect to a narrow conscience as to a great, so long as it is faithfully followed. If it is mere fidelity to conscience that is the chief thing, and not the contents of the conscience, or its word, then the little bigot who wrangles about trifles of ritual, or divides a Church upon an item of accounts, may be as faithful to his lean conscience as the large-minded, full-souled preacher who risks the displeasure of the public and the loss of his living for startling them with a great new Gospel. If it is a mere case of fidelity to conscience, you must pay as much honour to Laud with his formal piety and his mechanical churchism as to Luther with his vast living soul and faith. When a great conflict is going on we cannot stop to listen to the little moderates who think we are too severe because Mr. So-and-So is a most conscientious and devoted man. Of course he is. We take that for granted and go on. It is the conscientious men that are most worth fighting. It is the conscientious men that do so much mischief, the men who are more concerned about being true to their conscience than about their conscience being true to truth and right. Many of the men most dangerous to mankind have been conscientious men, apostles of the canonical conscience, like Laud, who have sincerely believed that without their machinery the world would go to perdition, led there by the Nonconformists with a conscience equally supreme. I should have no difficulty in believing this to have been the conviction of Torquemada the inquisitor, who was so much more thorough with Laud's principles and his conscientious cruelty than Laud's time allowed him to be. The exterminators may be as conscientious as the persecutors—they are much more logical and effective. There have been heroes of the conscience on the Catholic side as on the Evangelical, and there are to-day. There may be as many, there may be more. We do not judge individuals or count them, and therefore we do not need to ask whether they were conscientious men or not. We deal with principles and gospels.

Wherefore, the great question is what the *contents*

of the conscience were, or are; not how the man held to his conscience, but how his conscience held to reality, revelation, and truth. Luther's merit was not the heroism of his conscience, but the rediscovery of a new conscience beyond the natural, and beyond the institutional—whether canonical in the Church, or civil in the State. He found a conscience higher and deeper than the natural, the ecclesiastical, or the political—the individual, the canonical, or the civil; more royal than culture, clergy, or crown. He found a conscience within the conscience. He found anew the evangelical conscience, whose ideal is not heroism at all, but the humility and obedience of the conscience itself, its lostness and its nothingness except as rescued and set on its feet by Christ, in whom no man is a hero, but every man a beggar for his life. Luther had no sense of humility in regard to the Church of his day, the empirical Church anywhere; against it he stood for the rights of the individual. This was where he went beyond Augustine, with whom he had so much in common, and did for the Pauline Gospel what Augustine could not do, because possessed with a false idea of the Church and of the humility due to it. Against the institutional, hierarchical Church of Augustine Luther stood up, with a colossal independence, for the individual. But the independence was much more than colossal, and the courage was more than sublime. It was solemn, because subdued. It was not for the independent individual that Luther stood, but for the humbled, broken, crushed individual, new-made in Jesus Christ, and found in Him. The whole meaning of the Reformation was not so much that the individual was put in a new relation to the institution, but that he was put in a new relation to God and to himself. The Church as a necessary mediator of that relation was pushed aside. The whole Church system of forms and deeds, which centuries had built up till the sky was opaque and God remote, was swept out of the way. The intention was not to sweep it away, but only out of the way—to sweep it aside, and let men see Christ crucified. It was not to be swept out of existence, but only out of the path. The Reformation was not the assertion of the unchartered individual, but of the individual's right to a gracious God ; the right not of the natural freeman, but of the freeman in Christ ; not of the stalwart, but of the humbled and redeemed. The free conscience was a conscience bound inly and utterly to Christ alone.

III

It is well that the real and solemn nature of the Reformation individualism should be understood. It was not a thing to be snatched at, but a responsibility, and a heavy one. It was a calling in life—a calling of God. The individualism which is claimed as a right is common enough; we do not so often find it accepted as a calling, and construed as a duty. Luther's individualism was not the rejection of a burden, but its transfer from the outward Church to the inner soul. The vast spiritual problem of the medieval Church was removed from the broad arena of the Church, with its corporate conscience, and transferred to the interior of the single soul, to the conscience alone with judgment, and it was fought out in purely spiritual terms. The conflict of the soul had been much mitigated for the individual when it was conducted on his behalf by the Church at large; but the Reformation forced it in upon the isolated being whose eternal life was at stake, and he was made to feel it so intolerable that he rushed into the new truth with a breathless gratitude—born, indeed, of faith, but cradled in despair. The whole problem of the world was condensed into the experience of the single soul; and it was an experience in which his eternal salvation or damnation was at stake. In his narrow space the great spiritual deeps were broken up with sometimes volcanic force, and the eternal winds and waves roared in his being like the sea storm in the chimney of a cliff. The old helps of the Church were now useless; they had been found wanting. They had satisfied many of the best, but they were powerless even for the common sinner now, when the issue was sharply placed before him. The Church system of grace had been the slow ascent and purification of the soul through sacramental stages, the gradual education of the human into the divine; but this no longer sufficed. A sharp, unsparing contrast was set up in the soul between God's demand and man's fulfilment; the failure was carried home, and with it man's impotence to mend his case. If salvation was to come, it must come direct from God; and it must come as an immediate and final possession, not as a slow and perilous process. All natural development was here broken short; all spiritual culture, as mere culture, was ineffectual for the fiery crisis. It must be cut short by instant action and decisive change, and the new hope must flow from a miracle of God in the soul. And that was the nature of faith. It was a miraculous peace brought by God out of an intolerable war, which was desolating the soul in a way no Church could stay or cure. The battle, therefore, was no more fought on the broad plain of a Church's experience, nor was the authority for the conscience sought in a community. To commit the great holy war to a corporate Church tends to blunt the spiritual sensibilities of the man, and enfeeble his spiritual tone. All was now transferred to the narrow area of a personality, with its infinite and eternal spiritual issues. But to transfer such an awful conflict there, and then to leave it without such aid as the Church had striven to give, was more than the soul could bear. It would have snapped and perished in the strain, it would have been ground up in the clash and pressure, but for the fact that within the man's personality a new Personality stood with healing in His hands. In the furnace walked the Son of Man. Where the Church had stood like a baffled wizard at a magic circle beyond his spells, and vainly tried to enter the real area of strife, there stood now the Redeemer—stood suddenly in the midst, and said, "Peace be unto you," and there was peace. The individual did not become the authority which the Church used to be, but he did become the sphere in which another authority in another personality arose to reign; the individual did become the area of revelation which the Church had been. In a religion everything turns on the nature of the revelation. The religion is just what the revelation makes it, because religion is just the faith that the revelation evokes and that answers it. What was the Christian revelation? A system or an act? a theology or a redemption? a visible Church or a spiritual reformation? a truth or a person? grace as the capital with which God set up the Church in business, or grace as His act on the individual soul? The whole question between Protestant and Catholic turns on the nature of revelation. While to the Catholic it came as a system, to the Protestant it came as a salvation. It came as personal redemption, it became revelation only as redemption, and within the soul arose another soul to be its true King and Lord. The only truth for the soul was not Redemption but its Redeemer. What was revealed was not truth in the custody of a Church, but it was a spiritual act and person of salvation in the experience of a soul. That was the nature, the price, the glory of the individualism of the Reformation. If it discarded a Church, it was not in self-will, as the mindless thought and think, but it was to take up an awful conflict and a solemn charge. The Church could never carry that charge when the soul really came to feel itself and its sin, but only the Church's Lord and Saviour could in the soul's own secret centre and sacred shrine.

IV

Luther was certainly not a champion of the Renaissance, of the new learning with its new claim for intellectual freedom, of the new culture with its new sense of human reason, human thought, human beauty, and human grace. The man that stood for that in the Christian name was Erasmus, the true type of the English Reformation—Erasmus, who thought that nothing more than mere reform was required, which should be in the hands of men of learning and position, pious scholars and gentlemen. When Luther appeared, these humanists rejoiced greatly, and saw in him a precious ally—as some of the best Pharisees greeted Christ Himself, and thought He might go far in their cause; as culture of many kinds welcomes Christianity for an agent of culture, of order, learning, art, literature, and gracious life. The universities always tend to treat Christianity rather as a culture than as a gospel, as one of the faculties than as life itself. But as Luther went his way, the humanists, the cultured people, almost all fell away from him; as the orderly and institutional Pharisaism had to renounce Paul and counterwork him. They found in Luther another spirit—not a reform, but what amounted to a new religion. And culture fell back, as culture always tends to do, into the institutional arms of some kind of Catholicism, devoid of the bold, perilous, original, and searching evangelical note. Luther was not an organ of the Renaissance, but of a mightier movement, in which the Renaissance itself was to find its true destiny, and win the victory it had not power with the soul to gain.

V

Luther was not a champion either of the conscience or of the reason, but of the Gospel. He was not so much a moral figure as a religious. His work was for faith more than for morality, for religion more than for the conscience, and for the conscience as lost rather than for the conscience as king. Luther did what Augustine had tried and failed to do for the reason I have named. He restored Christianity from the Church to religion; he made faith once more a religious thing. His key-word was not law and order, it was not even righteousness and piety; it was grace. And it was answered not by the mind's assent, nor by amendment of life, but by a new life altogether, a new kind and principle of life, the life of faith. He did free men from the letter of Scripture, from scholastic theology, from the authority of the Church; but that was done incidentally to the great deliverance he was charged with—the gospel of the soul's deliverance from guilt. What made him groan in his monk's cell was not the bondage, tyranny, narrowness, immorality of the Church, but the burden of his own soul, his own self, his own guilt. It was the load of guilt that was killing him, not the load of the Church. He turned on the Church only when he found that it could do nothing real and final for misery and sin. It could not only do nothing, but it stood in the way of anything being done. Luther did not set out to save men from the tyranny of the Church, but from the guilt and death of sin; and he saved them from the

Church by the way, because the Church pretended to save them and could not. His ideal was not emancipation, but redemption; what he resented at the outset of all, and the root of all, was not man's tyranny over man, but man's tyranny over himself. And the Reformation never falls into discredit but when men are too proud, worldly, or well off to feel the moral load of their own souls, or the need of being delivered from their own guilt. It is easy to agitate against an outward tyrant—easy by comparison. It is not easy —it is far too hard for any but a few—to agitate against the tyrant in themselves, and fight for that inward freedom which the Gospel alone can give. When you hear tell of the simplicity of the Gospel and the lightness of its yoke, remember these words, "Except your righteousness, your Christian ideal of righteousness, exceed the laborious righteousness of scribe, priest, and Pharisee, ye cannot enter the Kingdom of Heaven." The simplicity of Christianity is very searching and very severe.

VI

The severity of the Gospel was for Luther so great that it broke the soul to pieces and ground it to dust to make the new man. The Church was severe in a way, and its way to perfection was laborious; but it was an unsearching severity, spread thinly over a wide area of life. It was split into a multitude of demands, observances, mortifications, persecutions of human nature. It was ascetic severity. The severity of the Gospel is pointed; it goes to the heart; it is the severity of a sword; it is concentrated, intense, deadly. It is thorough with the old man and his sin, as it is thorough with the new man and his salvation. Luther's work, while it made faith simpler in one way, yet made it much more hard, exacting, and powerful than it had been before. It was the simplicity of concentration, which is intense and irresistible. Luther's work was one of concentration from functions to acts, from acts to the soul. He compelled religion from acts which were mere offices to an act which taxed the whole will and soul, the decisive act of faith and its surrender. His work was a vast concentration; as it withdrew religious effort from a wide range of detailed conduct, it made it converge upon the central man in such a way that the amount of his religion was changed into its quality. There are substances that under intense pressure lose their former constitution, as it were, and from an expansive gas become a condensed fluid. They liquefy under pressure. So with the work of Luther's Gospel; the soul liquefied under its concentrated pressure, and became as it were another nature. The extent of its religion, being compressed from works to faith, was changed into a new kind of religion. What had been a volume of outward observance became a drop of spiritual power. Luther called in the forces of the soul from the elaborate system of a Talmudic Church, with its penances, asceticisms, precepts, ordinances, and canons, and he fixed them on a single infinite point. He effected a huge simplification, while he made the one new thing far more searching and imperious than the variety of the old. It was easier to trust God than do the penances of the Church; yet it was harder, because the whole moral will must bow, and not merely the outward consent. Humble and sure trust in God's fatherly forgiveness and care in Christ was drawn forth from under a heap of refined and complicated regulations, like a jewel from the débris of a great fire. Luther took it and set it in the forehead of the Church, and made it the very eye of religion and life's ideal. He took faith, which had been a system of mere compliance, and he made it the simple but arduous act of the soul's penitent obedience to the Gospel of God's forgiving act, and deed, and promise in Christ. Grace became a mercy exercised by God on the soul through faith's act, and not an influence infused by the act of a sacrament. Christianity becomes outwardly Christ, inwardly faith. Its key-word is not so much sanctity or inspiration as forgiveness. The forgiven man is the saint, not the consecrated monk. Not piety so much as trust, not ecstasy but confidence, not sweetness but power becomes the religious ideal—power unto God, and power over the world—power, by the reconciliation with God, to be reconciled with hateful and hating men, and to serve, in Christ, men to whom naturally we would not bend an inch from our way. The meaning, nature, and place of faith were changed. It became the permanent essence of religion. It had been the mere assent to absolution, it was now the soul's response to forgiveness; from self-surrender to the Church it became self-committal to Christ; from compliance with the canonical regulations it became the obedience of the total man to the Gospel; from opinion or achievement, as preliminary conditions leading to something greater than faith, it became the trust than which nothing is greater, because it trusts all the love in the world in the fatherly love and salvation of God.

VII

Let us pursue Luther's principles in more detail. How did he work out that new idea of faith and the perfect godly life? Especially, how did this idea of faith affect the Church? He had two things—a *foundation* which was God's Word, and a *power* which was man's faith.

1. He believed that it was the Word of God that *founded* the Church. The Church was not based on

tradition, nor upon bishops and popes. These were too variable, too unsure. Yet it did rest on something fixed, something objective, something given to man and not contributed by him. It rested upon no invention, but on a revelation; not on an achievement, but on a gift. The act of Christ which founded the Church was, in its very nature, above all a gift of God to man. Christ's work was much more a gift of God to reconcile man than a gift of man to reconcile God. The Church rested on this gift of God—upon something which had always been there, though obscured and perverted—always there as the true reality of the Church. It was now open to all, to the simplest, to every Christian as Christian, in virtue of his faith. It was not to be opened by pope, or bishop, or council, or saint; nor could they close it, and shut out men of faith. The foundation of the Church was there in the Bible, when interpreted in its actual, original, spiritual sense, apart from allegory and from any outside authority. In a word, the foundation of the Church was the Gospel, and the Church is the fellowship of the faithful, to whom the Gospel is Gospel indeed. It is easy to see how the Independent idea or gathered Churches, as distinct from territorial, flows from this. The Gospel is thrust into mankind as a magnet into a heap of iron dust and sand; and the Church is composed of the particles that cling, organized by the movements of the magnetic force.

VIII

2. This gospel was the true Word of God on which the Church was based. The Word of God, at the base of His Church, was not any phrase spoken by Christ founding a Church, nor an instruction or commission to the apostles. HE *is* the Church's one foundation; it is no edict or commission of His. Christ *did* very little (some say nothing) in the way of founding a Church; but He *was* everything. The Church proceeded from His work and person, not from words He said. It stood on what He was and is, and not upon what He devised. It stood and stands on the Gospel. And by the Gospel is meant, not a book, or a system, or a scheme, but the very act, deed, and revelation of God in Christ. The Gospel is not truth about God's reconciliation; it is God Himself reconciling in Christ. The Gospel is God in Christ, God in His Cross, God in Redemption. The permanent Gospel is the base of the permanent Church, and the permanent Gospel is the eternal Christ in the heaven of redeemed experience. This Gospel creates its own answer, and that answer is faith, and so we come to Luther's *power*—faith. The Word of God has been conceived at various times to be the letter or

the Bible, or the Bible as a whole, or the doctrines running through it, or the promises scattered in it. For Luther it was the vital principle of the Bible, the long act of revelation and Redemption which the Bible records—the Bible's heart and power; in a word, Jesus Christ and Him crucified. The testimony of Christ is the spirit of Scripture. No statement can save, no precept, no doctrine, no law; not the sweetest, comfortablest doctrine can save as doctrine, as mere truth; only the truth as Jesus. Only a person can save a person. A Church cannot, for it is a system, an institution. And no institution has saving power. It can serve salvation, but it cannot either save or damn. What the soul needs is Gospel, and an institution is law. To grasp the distinction between law and gospel, to grasp that with true insight, is to grasp the real core of religion and the clear nature of faith. It is because Christian people do not grasp this difference, and do not therefore realize the true nature of faith, that the empirical Church is the formidable thing it is to-day. A Church is more of the Law than of the Gospel, and the more powerful it grows the more is it a menace to faith. What must control the Church, in actual practice and not mere theory, is the Word of God as the Gospel coming to the soul through faith, with the Church as a mere herald and medium and agent. Rob faith of its place and power, and the Church becomes not a medium but a mediator, its minister becomes its priest, and its policy is not service but power. Faith is fatal to such a place for the Church. It is direct dealing of the soul with Christ. Christ is the object of faith, not a book, or a Church. Faith is taking Christ's forgiveness seriously and heartily. The devils or the wicked could believe in the Church (for Churchmen have been both); but the one thing they cannot believe in is the forgiveness of sin (else they would cease to be devil or damned); and, therefore, this is faith's distinction from the world and hell. The true authority over the soul and conscience is given through this faith. That authority is not the Church, but it is the effectual Word of God in the preaching of the cross, to which the conscience owes its life. And doctrine is just the best account we can give of this living faith in its living community.

IX

This faith, then, was the new, the reformatory thing in Luther's position. What did it replace? It replaced what we find passing for religion to-day in the circles where the Reformation influence has not truly penetrated, where an institutional, episcopal, and priestly Church keeps the public soul under a mere Catholicism. What is that? What is the idea of religion current in the semi-reformed circles of this country to-day? What is the idea of religion that the man in the street can be made pugnacious, and even furious, about when it is assailed? What is the shape into which his vague education has cast his natural religiosity? It is the Catholic idea of certain beliefs and certain behaviours; of accepting the knowledge of God and of the world authoritatively given by the historic Church of the land, along with the exercise of certain moral virtues to correspond; 'Believe in the Incarnation and imitate Christ.' That is all very well, but it is not a Gospel, only a Churchspel. Orthodoxy of creed and of behaviour is this ideal, rising to the idea of imitating Christ as the great Example, but too seldom tending to trust Him as a matter of direct personal experience. It is right knowledge on the Church's authority, and right conduct in personal relations, but less of actual and experienced personal relations with the divine object of the knowledge. Now the Reformation did not discard either right knowledge or right conduct; but it cast these down, for their own sakes, to a second place; and it put in the first place what Catholicism had, for the average believer, only made second (if second)—the personal trust and experience of Christ in a real forgiveness. Out of that all right belief and conduct must proceed, and it was the only guarantee for either. The first was made last and the last first. The whole Reformation might be defended as a crucial instance of that characteristic principle of Christian change, of divine judgment by inversion. The thing that was now put first is the thing that is always first in the spiritual order. It is the creative thing. Faith is the power creative both of right creed and right living. All the ethical world spreads away from the true focus of personal faith in God's forgiving grace in Christ. All the moral order is ruled from this throne. I do not say that morality does not exist apart from religion; it does. But I do say that finally it cannot; in the spiritual and ultimate nature of things the two are not separable, distinguish them as you may. The permanent ethic is Christian ethic; and Christian conduct dies soon after Christian faith.

The new thing, therefore, in Luther's Christianity was really the religious understanding of the Gospel. It had been understood, theologically, ecclesiastically, morally before, though not properly understood. It was never properly understood till it was understood religiously, by faith alone, by the lost soul saved. That was Luther's starting-point and goal alike. All his work began in this, and it was all for the sake of this. It was only gradually that it was forced on him how incompatible with this was Catholicism, the Church habit of mind, the Church idea of faith, the

Church claim on obedience, the Church's position as mediator between God and man, the Church custom canonized, the Church staff idolized, the ministry sacerdotalized, and administration made hierarchy. He did not mean a new Church. The new Church only arose by the resistance of Catholicism to faith, to religion, by the obstinacy of the canonical conscience to the evangelical. A new Church really arose because what Luther brought from the New Testament was a new religion. Catholicism is not so much another form of Christianity as another religion. It rests ideally though not empirically on a totally different idea of faith, and that is what makes a religion. Protestantism saved Christianity for religion, saved it as a religion, saved it from becoming a mere institution. To religion, Catholicism, Roman or Anglican, is at last fatal, as continental atheism shows. And failure to see that is due less to want of vision than of insight, to lack not of ability but of the intuition or faith, and the witness of the Spirit. It was the Holy Spirit that made Protestantism, more than Luther, Calvin, or Melanchthon. Or, if we put it in the diluted language of modern thought, it was made by the genius of Christianity. It was Christianity reforming itself. It was the victory of the instinct of self-preservation in Christianity.

The Reformation was the work of Christian faith

coming to itself, much more than the work of single men or groups. The faith made the men, not the men the faith. It was the self-assertion of the true Christian idea—not its assertion, but its self-assertion. It was not something that men spoke; it spoke in men. Nothing on earth could have prevented such a movement, amid the perversion and inversion which faith had undergone in the course of Catholic centuries. Catholicism is quite incompatible with the New Testament idea of faith as Luther rediscovered it; and a decisive issue was bound to come then as now. The two ideas destroy each other; they certainly could not both be supreme in the same house. A mere institutional faith could not claim to be the saving faith in any Church which possessed, honoured, and *understood* the New Testament. The Catholic and the Evangelical ideas of faith are incompatible, because each claims to be absolute. The priest of the sacraments has no room for the minister of the Gospel; the ministry of the Word has no place for the vicarious priest. A faith in which any human priest is essential is utterly incompatible with one in which the priest is a peril and a treason. And this is not human self-will; it is the antipathy of two mutually destructive ideas, the process of a historical and spiritual logic.

X

You hear politicians say that the Church must be comprehensive, and that the High Church party has as good a right to its place within it as the Evangelical. How it may be as to parties I know not, but it is quite certain that the High Church idea, in so far as it is sacerdotal, can have no room nor tolerance for the other. If the true minister of Christ is a priest, then his business must be to remove from the Church all ministers who are not priests. If the Catholic idea of faith is right, it is supreme and sole, and there is no room over its head, or by its side even, for the evangelical idea of faith, which is bound to be equally absolute in its claims. Two absolutes cannot sit on the same throne or rule the same Church. This, of course, supposes that the Church is something prior to the State, higher than the State, existing in its own right, and living entirely on its own faith. It supposes that the Church is a spiritual unity, pervaded by the one Spirit, and based on one consistent idea of faith, which it is free to give effect to, and bound both to obey and enforce. In such a Church, which is the true idea of a Church, the two orders of faith are not compatible ; and it is only obscurity or insincerity that can lead any sacerdotalist to say that his place in the

Church allows him to concede a like right and freedom to the Low Churchman if he will let him alone. But if the Church be not such a free body, if it be a Service of the State, in which the statesman's word is supreme, if it cannot give effect to its own principles and affinities, then I can understand the plea of comprehension. It is intelligible enough in men who know nothing whatever of the true genius of the Church, whose minds are incurably political, and who realize the spiritual situation on the historic scale so little that they think the same Church can house to-day the two ideas that rent Christendom in a strife that rent Europe. Two *parties* may dwell in the same realm and sit in the same house, and they may work well enough as political working goes. But the Church is not the State. The State has not an initial and positive charter, as the Church has, in the Bible. The Church is the sphere of revealed ideas. If its fundamental ideas are at feud it must be rent. The men might sit together, and do, and I hope always will, at dinner tables and philanthropies, and always in mutual respect for Christian character, or Christian learning, or Christian culture and honour. But the two ideas cannot lie down together. Their spheres and procedures are different. They cannot co-operate on opposite benches of the same house.

XI

The sphere of the Church was for Luther the region of faith. Its members were the people of faith. Only the believer knows the Church. Only the believer belongs to it; and not the believer in the Church, but the believer in Christ. The Church is not the object of faith but only its home. It does not produce faith, but it is the home where faith is born and brought up, where all things are ordered in the interest of faith. She is not so much the mother of the believer as his nurse. She holds the believer in her bosom, and he grows in her care. Faith is not faith *in* the Church—that is Catholicism—but faith *through* the Church. How shall they believe without hearing, or hear without preaching? and where is preaching without the Word, which is entrusted to the Church? Outside the Church indeed is no salvation; but it is outside the Church of the Word, not of the sacraments. Outside the Church means not so much outside its membership or baptism, but outside the range and influence of the Word that makes the Church by making Christians. What makes Christianity is not baptism but the work of the Gospel—of which Baptism is but one symbolic expression; it is no creative act.

This is the Reformation principle, though there were others of the Reformers in whom it had become more clear than it did to Luther, especially in respect to the sacraments.

I say little or nothing, you may note, of the destruction of superstition. The Reformer was there not to destroy superstition but to assert faith. Our protest to-day is too much *against* superstition and too little *for* living faith. The deeper our faith is, and the more adequate in its intelligence, the less likely we shall be to throw about charges like superstition, which may easily sound supercilious and certainly irritating.

Religion is faith. The Christian religion is Christian faith, and Christian faith is faith in Christ alone. The difference between the Catholic and the Evangelical Church, which is the great coming war, is a difference between the Catholic and the Evangelical type of faith, and therefore it is a difference as to the true nature of religion, of Christianity, and its practical, spiritual ideal. It is not a conflict of creeds in the sense of articles. It is a conflict of spiritual types. And it is not so much a conflict which shall expel the other, but which shall rule the other in the proper sense of the word rule, as influence and not domination. There is much in the Catholic ideal which faith would be the poorer to lose, so long as it is kept in its due place.

The idea of faith in Catholicism was twofold. For the layman it meant assent to the Church and its Creed—the acceptance of these as true, and outward submission to them. The state of the heart was a secondary matter. For the saint it was a mystic union with the Godhead, which had its chief expression in moments of insight, rapture, and ecstasy. Religion was regarded as a form of inspiration or divine indwelling, and its flower was the sanctity of the devotee who adopted religion as a profession. Lay assent and saintly mystic rapture were the two forms ot Catholic faith. The object of the sacraments was to aid that fusion of human nature with the divine which was regarded as the core and crown of sanctity in the Incarnation. The ideal relation of God to man was an indwelling, lifting the soul to the height of joy and calm. Neither God nor man was treated supremely as a will, but rather as a substance, and their union was a fusion rather than a reconciliation. The ruling thought was not revelation but inspiration, not the word to the will but the breath to the being. Peace with God was rather the subjective calm of a religious mood reached by great and ascetic effort, and very fugitive after all. It was monastic, quietist, undisturbed, a state of consciousness which was an object and end in itself.

It was the quest for this that engaged the soul of Luther in his cell; and it was upon this quest that the new light broke which, if it had not been the rediscovery of the New Testament idea, would have been a new revelation to the world, and Luther would have been the founder of a new religion. As it was, he was but the first real herald of it since the apostles, and especially since Paul. In Luther Paul came to life again. Faith was no longer to be the assent of the mind to certain truths, nor obedience to an institution, nor the enjoyment of mystic union and rapture; but it was trust, confidence, sonship with God. The foremost thing was not inspiration but revelation; not the indwelling of the divine nature but the perennial utterance of God's saving word in act and fact, and the whole man's answer to it in trust. What was that word? What was the revelation? It was grace, mercy, forgiveness in Jesus Christ, and in Him directly and alone. Faith was, as Melanchthon said, simply trust in God's mercy to the sinner in Christ. It was not fusion with God's nature even as love, it was not being sunk in the abyss of the divine, or filled to rapture with the inflowing of the Spirit. It was not the translation of the soul into a divine substance, man becoming God through God becoming man. It was not seeing God, or feeling Him, but trusting Him, committing one's self, one's sins, one's soul, one's eternity to God in Christ, on the strength of God's act and promise in Christ's redemption. It was not elation, rapture, ecstasy—it was confidence. It was answering a person, a gospel, not a system, or a divine infusion. Its peace was not the calm of absorption, of losing ourselves in the ocean of God's love, but the peace of believing, of forgiveness assured and foregone in Christ, and trusted even amid repeated and cleaving sin. It was trust in God's forgiveness, and in His providence, for every soul. It was the peace, not of seeing God in rapture, but of believing amid a world of temptation, misgiving, and self-accusation.

> I shall my fierce accuser face,
> And tell him Thou hast died.

It was the peace of justification rather than of communion. It was not a state of subjective consciousness but an assured relation of the will to a will, of a person to a person, of a present to a future. It was the peace of no condemnation rather than of no disturbance. It was not so much an experience as a standing act, attitude, and habit of the moral soul, the spiritual will. This faith often overcame experience and saved us from it; the experience might be troubled but the faith stood fast. It went out of the cloister into the world; and it proved its sanctity in the godly way in which it did the world's work rather than in the exquisite sensibility of the solitary to sacred things. A new type of sanctity and perfection arose, not confined to those who had the religious genius or religious leisure. The saint might be something very different from the professional religionist, the sweet pietist, or the recipient of the beatific vision. That form of religion was not denied, but it became secondary where, for more than a thousand years, it had been primary. Faith in inspiration became second, and faith in Redemption and providence became first. Sanctity was approved *in* our calling, not *outside* it, not on Sunday, not in our closet. Men came into direct contact with the revealed God by faith. This faith became the acceptable, the justifying thing. It was the universal priesthood, and the priest and the monk fell at one stroke from being the idols to be the servants of the Church—useful, possibly, but not indispensable. Neither priest nor saint commanded the grace or forgiveness of God. Nothing human, nothing in the nature of an institution, must come between the soul and its Redeemer, whether it were the system as a Church or the system as a creed. The Church was the community of the faithful; not of the episcopal nor of the sacerdotal, but of the souls in direct contact with the Saviour, and held to Him by the will's obedience and the heart's trust in the work of His Redemption. The Church was a witness, not a judge,—a medium, not a mediator; it might absolve but not forgive; it could convey a forgiveness which it could never effect.

XII

"Luther's central position was to identify faith with the assurance of salvation." These are the words of the greatest of modern historians of theology whose further remarks I will venture freely to paraphrase.[1]

The point of Luther's breach with Catholic piety was this. That piety kept putting the question: How am I, a sinful man, to get power to do good works? I cannot please God unless I do them, but do them I cannot to win my peace. To this question the Church gave its own answer; and a long-winded answer it was. It constructed a tremendous apparatus of satisfaction. It took the sufferings of Christ, the sacraments, and the débris of human virtue, faith, and love; and from these it compounded a system through which the sinful soul was passed, like the rags into a paper mill, to come out, after a long and terrible discipline, white and pure at the other end. Luther began with a totally different question. He did not ask for power to do things that would commend him to God; he asked for such a commendation to God as would enable him to be the right man with Him, and to do the right things as a consequence of that. His experience was the soul certainty through faith, once for all, that in Christ he had a gracious God. He described with

[1] Harnack, *Dogmengeschichte*, bk. III. ch. iv. § 2.

mighty joy the experience which God's grace had made him pass through. He knew that all true life and blessedness, in so far as they were his, flowed from this certainty of faith. It was the source of his sanctification, and all the good things he might do which were pleasing in God's eyes. For him the whole question about the relation of faith and goodness was simplified. He must grow in holiness. He must fight fearful spiritual foes with a most real and objective existence. And he must conquer. But when the battle threatened to go against him, when he felt he had no power in himself, when he must lay hold of some objective reality to withstand these real and objective foes, it was not at sacraments he grasped, not at the assurances of the Church, not at penances, and satisfactions, and merits of saints who had more than overcome. All these were not objects of faith, but reeds which grew on a shore *he* could not tread, and which broke in his desperate grasp as he was hurried on in his passionate way. When he flagged in his goodness, he grasped at the work and promise of his gracious God in Christ, and burst into the more passionate prayer, " Lord increase my faith." His assurance that he was a saved man was not the sense that he had complied with the statutes of a Church, sent for the prescriptions of the priestly pharmacopœia, and obeyed the advice of the Church's system of spiritual medicine. It was through his act of faith in the forgiveness of God reaching him directly in the Cross of Jesus Christ. This was the Alpha and Omega of Luther's Gospel as of Paul's. The old confession of the Church was : where there is knowledge of God there is life and peace. But there was no clearness to the self-analysing and dim-seeing soul as to which knowledge of God was meant. Was it some future knowledge, philosophic knowledge, intuitive knowledge, mystical sacramental knowledge, knowledge by the Logos, knowledge by effort ? On all these tracks men travelled and wandered, and the soul was still from home, weary, unsure, and desperate. Luther did not seek a knowledge, but found it given to his hand in God, in Christ, actually redeeming and reconciling him in his actual state of need. Where there was this forgiveness and this faith there was life, and peace, and joy.

This was the real nature of the breach with Catholicism that took place in the Reformation. It was not so much a new idea of the Church as a new idea and type of religion. It is the moral ideal of Protestantism that is its grand distinction from Catholicism. It is not so much the theology, but the ethical quality, the spiritual habit, that divides them. And the moral quality, the spiritual habit of the English people is the one and not the other ; to adopt the other would involve a total change in our national characteristics, our life ideal, and our religion and our place and function in the world. Catholicism is national suicide. I do not say political, but national. We should renounce not merely our prosperity, but our nature, our soul. I shall return to this. I would only ask here, What shall it profit a people if it gain the whole Church and lose its own soul?

XIII

Religion, then, is Faith. I state expressly here what I have often said in passing. Religion is Faith, and Justification by Faith is not a doctrine of Christianity, but its very nature and substance. The true sphere of religion is the sphere of faith. All that religion is able to do for love or hope can only be done as the development of what is in faith. Religion is not doing certain things, or obeying certain men, or leading a particular order of life. It is not ritual, not clerical, not monastic in its nature and genius. It is to be exercised in our natural and lawful calling in life, and especially in the trust of God's providence, and the service of our neighbour. It is the one thing pleasing to God and justifying to man. It was faith that redeemed, and it is faith that lays hold of redemption. It was Christ's faith that redeemed, and ours is but the trust of His. It is adaptable to every honest form of life—in marriage, the family, the state, in business, in society, in affairs. The one divine service is faith. The one morality is trusting Christ as a life obedience. All morality is folded up in that and expands from it. Divine service is not ritual, not mystic contemplation, not asceticism. If, then, ceremonies in themselves avail nothing, either for the soul or God, the only sphere of faith is life. Faith is a mode of life, and heart, and temper, an attitude of these towards Jesus Christ, a standing act and habit of will toward God. The moment you bind up with it any institution as an essential part of its object instead of a historical instrument, you have replaced Christianity by Catholicism, by the Church. You "bow down to your net and worship your own drag." You do as a nation does, when it worships the army, which is the law's instrument, above the law which should wield it and the people it should serve.

The Protestant revolution was not primarily in Christian theology any more than it was primarily directed against the Church; it was a revolution in the religious type, in the idea of the perfect life.[1] It was a moral and practical change. Catholicism breeds a different type of man from Protestantism—you might almost say a different type of face, certainly of conscience. Luther revolutionized the Christian idea of

[1] May I refer for detail to my little book on *Christian Perfection?* (Hodder & Stoughton, 1899.)

perfection, of the perfect life, as no Christian had done since the apostolic age. Perhaps this was the most central effect of all. The new idea of faith as a life meant that with the supremacy of a new faith there came a new ideal of life. Perfection was no longer a thing ecclesiastical, or even saintly, but moral, religious, humane, worldly in the godly sense. Neither priest, monk, nor nun was the religious ideal, but the man and woman among men in Jesus Christ. It was an immense revolution; every new ideal of life must be. It reopened the world to religion, to the believer. The new world of America, discovered just before, was not so new or vast as the new world now opened to the human spirit. We might say the one was discovered in order to be a refuge and a sphere for the other. Where would English faith have been without America to fly to? A vaster world dawned in all ways. There was more earth and more sky, a wider soil for a wider soul. The kingdom of God has something wider, humaner, more historic and profound even than the Great Church. Nature itself took a new meaning and consecration. Marriage and the family took a new place, and ceased to be only the best thing for an inferior sort who were not equal to the altar or the cloister. Freedom took a new meaning for the world and for nations as men were set free by faith and started on a new moral career. The future had a new light as men felt that they were redeemed from their past. The past itself ceased to be an accumulation merely or chiefly, a burden, a drag, a water-anchor on the race. When the kingdom of God and His righteousness were sought by faith in Christ, all else seemed added. Luther taught men and convinced men anew what true religion, true Christianity was; and in its wake came science, and the modern State with its civic and municipal life and social rights. The Church made the nation, especially this nation; but it was not the Church that made the modern State, and it would never have made it. Philanthropy became a public passion and a social duty, not the vocation of those who would be saints. It became an exercise of faith instead of an education for sanctity, the expression of the believer's love instead of the saint's ambition, an utterance of the Christian heart instead of an investment for the future of the soul.

XIV

Luther, I reiterate, rediscovered Paul and the New Testament. He gave back to Christianity the Gospel, and he restored Christianity to religion. But in giving us back the old he brought to pass the new age. He magnified the individual to himself, and so he opened a new world to the world. Catholicism was but half of life. It is a maimed and unmanly thing in its type after all. Any creed maims and fetters humanity which makes personal religion but a part of it, and ties its religion down to an organization. The human soul cannot be completely organized and remain infinite and divine. It can use an organization, but it cannot be reduced to organization. It cannot be comprehended in any institution, any Church. But Catholicism would so treat it; and the ideal is an outgrown Paganism, which the Reformation first broke. The ancient world reduced the soul to the State; the State was the supreme human interest. Catholicism did no more than apply the same Pagan and irreligious principle to the Christian soul; it made the soul's supreme interest to be the religious state, the Church. The old pagan idea did not really receive its deathblow till the Reformation. The new age, the new human career, then first broke out of the old faith when Luther brought that faith to light. The human race has a treasure in the Reformation which it has never truly realized; how much more of treasure has it in the New Testament! In Catholicism the whole of the man was not claimed for religion, for faith, but only a side, a part of him. He had to be pruned down in order to find the one great way to God, not filled out. When a saint was made a man was lost. He had to be cloistered, monasticized, mortified.

Whole fields of human energy had to be given up if mankind was to reach true holiness. But the Reformation made the saint an active citizen of the world because he was so much more. Yet he was not the lusty natural man. His freedom was not in himself, but in the grace of the whole world's God, the Redeemer of the whole soul. What the Reformation brought for the new great age was not naturalism any more than it was monasticism. The natural man was broken in the cross and its faith, but the heavenly man that was made was free of all the world, and had the reversion of all its powers, and all its future. Modern engineering is as truly, though not as directly, a product of the Reformation and its moral courage as modern philanthropy is. The faith of the new movement infinitely enhanced the energy, the confidence, the courage, the active power and joy of life. The world of nature became man's friend and ally where to the monk and his purity it had been damnation. Man could master nature without being lost in it. Neither ancient Paganism nor its Christian form, Catholicism, ever had a principle that reconciled man and nature, soul and sense. Nature was either declared by the mystic to be unreal, a mere fleeting show for our illusion; or it was reconciled with the spiritual by the priest, by a mere magical process like transubstantiation which carried with it no moral power over the world. There was what is called a dualism in the Catholic and pagan idea of man and nature—an intractable, unreconciled dualism which meant a constant (though only half-conscious) irritation to the soul, and a constant leakage of its power at the bad joint. Marriage, for instance, was not a sacred thing in itself; it was only made sacred by the blessing upon it of the Church. To separate from the Church was to put a stain and a ban on the continuance of the race. An unchurched race was a cursed race. Nature was not hallowed by Christ's redemption, except in so far as that was dispensed in the Church's blessing. To this dualism an end was made by the great simplifying principle of Justification by Faith alone. The world is a redeemed world; and Nature, the redeemed servant, waits, longs to be used by the son of the house, the man whose manhood and whose mastery are made by the same redemption.

When the great spiritual process was removed, as faith moves it, to the interior of the man's spiritual will, the new relation to God brought a new and trustful relation to His world. Nature was no more Satanic, lurking for chances to undo the soul. It was included with the whole creation in the same great final redemption to which the soul owed itself. The immense new strength with which the soul came out of its awful struggle with the ultimate powers of spiritual being greeted the vast powers that played in the natural world, and it knew itself their lord. For Catholicism, with its starvation of the soul's power, and its substitution of the calm of mere order for the peace of power, this was impossible. Catholicism, tied and galled by the absolute rule of a Church institution, like Gulliver by the Liliputian packthreads, could never let the human soul find its feet on faith. And Catholicism, if it were to return on England, would in course of time reduce it from the most free, adventurous, powerful and righteous nation on the earth to the timid, vainglorious, petulant, cruel, pleasure-loving and bankrupt race which it has made Spain. Catholicism would do this—not popery merely, but Catholicism, which hampers the soul by the worship of an institution, debases it by the prying of the priest, enfeebles it by the priest's false promise to take the responsibility of its fate, and prunes down energy by an incessant and suspicious vigilance against every new departure that takes the soul beyond the Church's right, reach, and control. Catholicism is the sacrifice of the soul to an institution ; Protestantism is the soul's release for an institution. And the issue is this, is the soul for the Church, or the Church for the soul ?

XV

If we take Catholicism as religious institutionalism, its most serious danger to society is the moral one. It affects the standard of honesty, then of honour, and it becomes Machiavelism. The conscience was never meant to have for its authority anything in the nature of an institution, but only a person to whom its relation is faith; and if for this person is substituted a system of any kind, not all the good and gentlemanly instincts can prevent the conscience from ultimate perversion and decay.

It has often been pointed out how the Catholic movement affects the quality of *religion*, how religion tends to sink under its influence by ceasing to be experimental and personal. It might be shown how the very self-searching of the confessional destroys the real power of self-examination, and cultivates a levity in regard to the nature of sin by an excessive attention to the numbers and the penalties of sins. This decay of real experimental religion (which is but a roundabout way of saying faith) is really a decay in the sense of sin. It is not a decline in the notice sin receives, but it is a debasement of the idea of sin by the intrusion of a wrong standard. That is sin which the Church declares to be so; what is not so declared is not sin. Such at least is the lay

WHAT DID LUTHER REALLY DO? 161

and popular inference. And it is in the lay mind that this religious mischief from Catholicism chiefly takes effect. The effect on the clergy, we shall see, is different. The effect on the laity is the decay of experimental religion. While the Broad Church tends to reduce sin to a mere ethical phenomenon, the Catholic tendency is to treat it æsthetically, or, what is the same thing, institutionally. It is what the conscience looks at rather than feels, and it measures it by an external standard supplied rather than realizes it by its own sensibility. The moral product of the Church system is the canonical conscience, which has its representative in what I have already alluded to as the narrow and inhuman sincerity of a man like Laud. To such a conscience sin is a very different thing from what it is to the Evangelical conscience, and far less of a religious thing. It becomes a social enormity. If an institution lace the whole sky through which God looks on the soul, it is inevitable that offences against God should be chiefly construed in an ecclesiastical or social way. The standard in a Catholic Church, especially when it is an Established Church, bound up with the social conventions of the country and its ruling class, becomes mainly conventional. The traditional social code becomes interwoven with the traditional ecclesiastical code, and both come for the public to form the standard of moral judgment, and even of such self-examination as can survive so hostile an air. The sense of sin becomes feeble, and the tone of religion outward and shallow. Ideals fall, and the existing Church becomes the best Church. It ceases to be thought of except as a branch of the national service, or a part of the social fabric. Genuine wonder is felt that any should regard it otherwise. So to view it seems an act of national treason, and hostility to society. This is, of course, the Pagan idea; and we can easily understand how persecution arose, not as an attack on religious views or practices in themselves, but as acts of self-preservation on the part of society against what was supposed to be an assault on its organic existence. Village persecution still is more social than religious in its inspiration. And "the plea for a State Church," says Dr. Dale, "draws its force from the disposition of men to think of the Church as being nothing more than a great human organization for maintaining Christian learning and propagating religious truth, or for civilizing mankind and improving the morality of nations." That is to say, there has come to pass, through the ecclesiastical and the political Catholicizing of the Church, through its institutionalizing (if we may use the word), a fatal severance between the idea of the Church and the idea of Redemption. And direct faith is dissociated from the personality whose contact with us is the real source of the due sense of sin. If we ask indeed why England is not Pagan to-day, the grateful answer must be : Because of the Church. But if we go on to ask why she is but half Christian, the answer, if critical and honest, must still be : Because of the Church, and especially because of the Establishment.

But there is another effect of the growth of Catholicism or religious institutionalism, which I said above was the more serious. It is the decay of the sense of honesty. And it is the form which most affects a clergy. By dishonesty is not, of course, here meant conscious turpitude, but such a sophistication of the moral perceptions that men come with elaborate sincerity to allow themselves in positions and practices which are open to the censure, not of the Christian conscience merely, but of the rude integrity of the world. It is not easy to resist this impression after the publication of Mr. Walsh's book. It certainly cannot be denied that a very great change has taken place in the conscience of the English clergy in the last half century. The Broad Church treatment of the formularies has often exposed the clergy to the criticisms of business men. But however preparatory this may have been for a more advanced stage of sophistication, it is nothing compared with the effect in that way of the principles of Tract 90. And all this is the inevitable result of Institutionalism. It is Machiavelism. It is the erection of the canonical conscience in the place of the Evangelical. Whether it be the ecclesiastical canons of Laud or the political canons of Bismarck that are enthroned, the effect of the canonizing is the same. It is moral sophistication, due to placing over the conscience a bureau where there should be a spiritual king. And the reaction against it is either the Reformation, or what is to-day called the Nonconformist Conscience. There have been extravagances in both, and, of course, to an institution-worshipper extravagance is the sin of sins. But none the less they have been, and are, the self-assertion for each age of that Puritanism, with its living faith, which is the nerve of vital godliness, and the conservator of moral progress in public and private life.

The whole of Europe is suffering from this institutional and Machiavelian strain, this corruption of conscience by empire, political or ecclesiastical. In the modern enhancement of human force, freedom, and passion the need is felt for some strong outward authority, which the general decay of faith yet forbids to be of a truly spiritual nature. Vast organizations are called in to govern a human nature which yet was constructed and redeemed to be governed only by the unseen King enthroned in moral faith. Defrauded of its true Sun, the conscience pines, shrivels, or dies. Its voice is silenced or warped. It becomes the tool of a visible organism which gives it its law, instead of the judge of a society whose law it should prescribe. And what is that but Machiavelism, which justifies all things in the name of an institution held supreme? It might be the army, as in France, where in the collapse of conscience even the sense of honour becomes criminal. It might be the State, as in Germany, where the Emperor seems to have no moral authority higher than his dynasty, and revives, in the name of a kind of theistic orthodoxy, the ancient Paganism of the worship of the State. The Machiavelism of Bismarck was open and avowed. All things were lawful which promised to subserve the interests of the State. Such ethic is more antichristian than any orthodoxy can redeem. It is the same thing that is expressed in the Socialism which is the enemy of the bureaucratic State. For the Socialist of the programmes all things are lawful which work the programme out, and the individual conscience has no more stand against the social State than the Emperor thinks it should have against his. Society takes the control of the conscience in the one case as thoroughly as the prince does in the other, and with less room, on the whole perhaps, for freedom than when the control is taken by the Pope. It is needless to remind you how, in the

Roman system now developed in the hands of the Jesuits, the Church as the religious society or institution claims a divine right to the control of the conscience in her own supreme interest. The Church, for its members, becomes the conscience of the priest, with results which in this country do not clearly emerge because of the corrections of a healthier moral inspiration. Jesuit ethics are the greatest system of moral Machiavelism that the world has seen. And wherever you have the spirit of ecclesiasticism winning the upper hand you have the like moral results in proportion. You have crooked and secret methods. You find done by well-bred men, and men of no bad feeling, on behalf of the Church things that they would not do as private gentlemen. You have men, who claim in Ireland that law should be obeyed loyally while it is law, going on to School Boards with the avowed purpose of hampering, if not neutralizing, the Education Act. You have the highest dignitaries capturing not only the schools for their Church but the charities which were left either expressly for another communion or expressly for undenominational purposes. You have gentlemanly men and their kindly women, whom it is a delight to meet in their own drawing-room, descending to acts of contemptuous persecution against the godliest of their Christian neighbours because of their crime as

Dissenters. It is hateful to speak of these things except as samples and as illustrations of the moral effect, especially on the clergy, of that institution-worship which is the soul of Catholicism and of Machiavelism alike. The constant tendency of Catholicism is toward Machiavelism. It is religion debased to a polity instead of using a polity, and being free to use a variety of them according to the discretion of faith. It is the debasement of empire infecting the great and sacred society which came into the world to save it from the condition to which the empires had brought it. It is the sophistication of the conscience by a system which came to save men from the sophistries into which all the systems had fallen. It is the capture of that inward freedom which came to be the guiding power of human freedom in every form. And the awful Armageddon which awaits Europe sooner or later will be due to those perversions of the conscience in Church and State which chiefly arise from taking it into the pay of an outward authority and institution; whose pay it must one day spurn and whose control it must disown if it is to remain human, progressive, and free.

XVI

Let us speak of England's national life and future alone. A leading statesman not long ago said that the secret of the British Empire lay not in the completeness of its constitution, nor in the omnipresence of its crown, nor in the ubiquity of its Parliament. For its constitution is full of illogical contradictions which are a working success; its crown has a very limited action at home, and a far more limited action abroad (except in the way of sentiment); and the arm of Parliament is a very short one when it is a question of action at the other side of the world. But the secret of the Empire is in the men whom Britain sends forth in their freedom, courage, mastery, and wisdom, in the resource and the responsibility developed by their having to act alone, without instructions, and without immediate supervision. It is not the English Parliament nor the English Constitution that is felt in the English proconsul on the skirts of the Himalayas, but the English *man*. All that is true. An empire like ours could not hang together for a century ruled simply as a magnificent and compact organization, and worked like a gigantic post office. But what does that mean? It means that our power is in its nature and genius Protestant and not Catholic, that its salvation is the development of individual resource and responsibility; that its doom would be to settle down into mere officialism, to set up the priestly idea of responsibility for the Protestant, and to regard the ideal Englishman more as a machine to obey orders than as a living moral centre of freedom, confidence, and power. Make our religion Catholic, and above all things institutional, and in due time you reduce English enterprise to something in the nature of a Jesuit mission, the Englishman abroad to a political cleric, the merchant to a retailer, and the great firm to the spirit of a tied house. That would in course of time be the result, if the type of English faith ceased to be Protestant and became Catholic. Our ideal of life would be ruled by the type which is pale, flat, meagre, and timid in the many, however ambitious, grasping, and domineering in the few. The type of pope and priest would stand out upon the slavish moral complaisance of the many. For it would be an article of faith to bow to the priest as a part of the soul's homage to God, to think of the priest as a minor god. And to the soul's faith both in itself and in God that is fatal, and it has been shown by the atheism of Catholic Europe so to be.

XVII

So do not think, when we speak of Justification by Faith alone, that something is meant which is intelligible only to those who are interested in theology. If we must be theologians to be Protestant, Protestantism is not what the world needs in the way of religion ; it is not evangelical. But Justification by

Faith is a great moral and spiritual principle. It is not what should be called a mere doctrine; it is a principle, type, way, and ideal of life. You must live on this principle or on its opposite, if you live a religious life, or any worthy life at all.

For Justification by Faith means three things of a very practical sort in our judgment of life:

1. It means that the worth of a man is to be measured exclusively by his moral and spiritual quality of soul, by his heart and character, by his direct faith in a moral and spiritual God; and not by his relation to any institution whatever, or his correctness in any creed. A man is to God not what he is to any Church, but what he is to God's real Word, will, and presence in Christ.

2. If this quality of soul, true faith, has the right object in a living Christ, it is bound by its very nature to take outward shape in hopeful and tireless moral energy, in righteous love and pity to other men, and in a Christian fellowship which is the sign and not the condition of faith. How can a faith which is personal contact with the Redeemer be any but a faith of practical justice, goodness, help, and blessing.

3. The value of the highest work does not depend on the form it takes or the results it wins, but on the faith which inspires it. All the energies of life are justified so long as they are capable of having this faith

put into them. They are not concreted by a Church which blesses them, or a priest who searches them and absolves, but by the spirit, motive, faith of the man who does them. In politics we are justified by results, in faith by motive. Law must regard actions, but faith regards souls. And to judge souls we must measure motives, and the motive of all motives is faith, as the test of all standards is Christ. Art itself is chiefly determined as great by its subject and not by its manner, by its content even more than by its form, by its faith more than by its technique, by its ideals even more than by its works.

XVIII

These are the principles of the modern man in his best and largest and humanest sense. They are the moral principles of modern civilization. The supremacy of faith means the supremacy of character. In Catholicism character is there for the sake of the Church; in Protestantism the Church is there for the sake of character. In Catholicism character is trimmed down to one type, dominated by the saintly ascetic; in Protestantism it is developed on individual and national lines, without the shadow of a universal institution which erases national features in its uniformity of type. In Catholicism we have a huge International which levels the nations under one uniform Church; in Protestantism, with the flexibility of faith, we have an International which develops the nation's native character as it does the individual's. Catholicism makes the nations tributary to itself; Protestantism makes them contributory to each other. In the one Faith rests on the Church, in the other the Church rests on Faith. In the one the Church is primarily the clergy, in the other it is the believer. In the one Faith means practically faith in the Church; in the other it is faith in Christ. In the one it is faith in what Christ is said to have appointed; in the other it is faith in what Christ in His person was and did, is and does. In the one it is faith in the grace that Christ spends; in the other it is faith in the grace that Christ is. In the one the work of Christ was to make the Church possible among men; in the other His work was to make man capable of a Church.

Luther believed in a Church, in a Church as founded by grace alone, in grace as mercy and not sacramental infusion, in grace as the Gospel, and in the Gospel as Christ Himself. Faith as the answer to revelation is the soul in direct contact with Christ crucified, not as the condition of grace but as Himself, the living, potent, *omni*potent, ubiquitous, eternal grace of God.

This is the faith of the New Testament, of the Gospel. It is not the faith of Catholicism, which is not the Gospel. In this faith let us stand. To do anything else is spiritual suicide. And indifference to the issue is one of the ways to this death; for you can kill yourself by a narcotic as surely as by a poison more acute.

THE REAL NATURE OF CHRISTIAN PRIESTHOOD

IV.—Part I

THE REAL NATURE OF CHRISTIAN PRIESTHOOD

I

THERE is nothing more earnestly desired by Christian men than the unity of Christendom, either in inward spirit or in outward form. And there is but one obstacle in chief which pushes in and forbids union. It is the priest. Between Catholic and reformed Christianity the priest is the real bone of contention. Between Anglican and Free Churchman the issue is the priest. It is a struggle on the one hand between the priest and the family; the priesthood means celibacy, and it means confession, and each of these is an assault on family life. The celibate priest means that marriage is on an inferior stage; and the confessor priest means his intrusion between the most intimate and sacred moral ties. It is a struggle, on the other hand, between the priest and the minister,—between the minister as a mediator, and the minister as an instrument; it is a struggle between the minister as a man, and the minister as something more than a man—which is in effect less. Catholicism, I have said, is that form of Christianity which raises an institution to an object of faith, and makes it essential to salvation. This institutionalism culminates in the priest. Catholicism is some form of priestism. In its extreme forms it not only makes the priest essential to the Church, but identical with it. Protestantism, as one has said, either abolishes the priest or multiplies him. It makes all priests or none. The priest means Judaism; and his reign means the relapse of Christianity into the religion it left behind. It is a reversion, which means degeneration. Something is seriously wrong with the principle, when we find the tendency with the priest, in practice, so steadily towards insolence, contempt, intrigue, and persecution, petty or great.

The priest was not in the apostolic faith, and he did not spring up in a night. He grew upon the Church, "built, like one of our cathedrals, through generations, in pieces, at long intervals, the development of a logic slow but sure from the false start."

The whole of this conception of an outward, ruling, and vicarious priesthood is a corruption of the Christian idea. It is a later importation. It is not in the New Testament. So far as human priesthood goes, there is nothing in the New Testament but the spiritual and inward priesthood of all believers—the universal priesthood of justification by faith. The justified are priests. The whole Church is a royal priesthood, a kingdom of priests. The word "priest" is deliberately avoided as a name for the Christian president or minister, though the air was full of it, and there was no religion in the world that the New Testament knew but called its ministers priests, and treated them so. Neither the name nor the thing is in the New Testament. It was too jealously monopolized for the person and work of Christ. The Church could have but one Priest, as the bride of Christ could have but one Spouse. Not one of the Apostles was a priest in this official and vicarious sense. They exercised neither mass nor confessional. They preached forgiveness, but they did not dispense it. Paul's forgiveness, in 2 Corinthians ii. 10, follows on that of the Church, " in the sight of Christ," not " in His name." The absolving power belonged to the Church, and it was not exercised in an express and formal way, but by the spiritual and releasing action of the Church's practical influence on the world's soul. Christ was no priest in this Catholic sense. His affinities were with the old prophets of Israel more than with the priests. These became His enemies and murderers ; and it was not because they were bad men, but because they were, before all else, officers of a monopolist institution—a Church. For some time the Church held this priestless faith of the common priesthood. Tertullian says (about 200 A.D.), "Where there are three there the Church is, if they be but laymen." And Augustine says, "All are priests as members of the one Priest." And many similar passages could be quoted from the Fathers of the Church.

But, meantime, the Pagan influences of the Roman world were at work in the Church. As it mastered the world outwardly, the world was corrupting it inwardly. The heathen idea of priesthood returned on the pure Christian faith like a tide; and this tidal force was aided, though it was not originated, by the strong current setting in the same direction from the Old Testament. In the third century there arose a powerful and thoroughgoing man who gave effect to these influences, and fastened the magical and theurgic priesthood upon the neck of the Church from that time forward. I mean Cyprian, Bishop of Carthage, the Laud of the early Church. He did for the priest what Ignatius, in the second century, had done for the bishop. The official and dominating priest from henceforth pushed the universal priesthood in practice out of sight. Yet it could not be entirely slain; it was bound up too closely with the vital nature of Christianity. So long as the Church remained Christian at all this principle was bound to struggle for life and scope. And so late as Thomas Aquinas, the greatest of all the Catholic theologians in the thirteenth century, we have this : " A good layman is joined to Christ in spiritual union by faith and love, *not by the sacramental power* ; so he has the spiritual priesthood for the offering of spiritual sacrifices." We shall see that, even at the Council of Trent in the sixteenth century, part at least of this idea remained and received expression. But it was only a theological expression. The practice of the Church had hardened considerably, as we shall note. In practice the official priesthood had submerged the universal, as in the Roman Church it does at this day ; and the only real and effectual assertion of the believer's priesthood in Christendom was, and is, Protestantism. The Reformation was the rescue of the universal priesthood of the Church from the official. And it found its only safety in doing what the New Testament writers had done—in banishing the name " priest " as the title of the Christian minister. The Anglican Church alone, with its want of earnestness and thoroughness, with its lack of spiritual " lucidity " (as Matthew Arnold would have called it), retained it; *hinc illæ lacrymæ* ; we have the troubles of to-day. We have that most ominous breach in a Church—

between its clergy and its laity. We have the clergy in the main Catholic, the laity in the main Protestant. We have each side representing an order of faith which is incompatible with the other. This must be a far more serious thing than the existence of two such *parties* in the Church. And the explanation of it, as we shall find, is that the Anglican priest, while resting on a representative theory of the ministry, yet applies it in such a roundabout way that only some of the ministers themselves grasp it, and none of the laymen. The authority of the apostolic succession through bishops is dragged in, and qualifies the representative nature of the priest in such a way that the lay priesthood cannot feel itself represented in the official priest at all. In our elective ministry it does.

II

But supposing we keep the name as describing the nature and privilege of every Christian man, the question I would ask is, What is the real nature of Christian priesthood? What is the nature and meaning of the priest for us—for us of the Free Churches? Whatever is the real nature of the priesthood is something which belongs to the Church as Christian, and not merely as sectional. It belongs to all Christians. When we reject the Catholic priest, we do not reject the priesthood. How can we? It is a priest that we worship in Christ. The Church, as the body of Christ, must in some sense express His priesthood. Priesthood, as the Roman catechism truly says, is the highest dignity on earth. It must be so if it was the great function of Christ. Priesthood, rightly understood, is the true seat of authority among men.

I shall begin with the admission that the true Church is in its nature sacerdotal. That is a truth which many of us have entirely lost, and we owe much to the present High Church movement for forcing it home upon all the Churches alike. To the loss of it is due most of our failure to reach and influence the world. It is priesthood that saves the world—the priesthood of Christ, and the real fellowship of it by the Church which His priestly act founded, and in whose action its High Priest lives for ever. The Church which the Great High Priest inhabits and inspires must be a priestly Church.

The confusion is caused when we cease to think that the Church *is* a priesthood, and begin to think that it *has* a priesthood. It is like the error the evangelicals make (so full of practical mischief to religion) when they say that man *has* a soul, instead of saying that man *is* a soul.

The main question is whether the essential priesthood of the Church is confined to a certain order of

Christians. Is the Church a priestly Church because it possesses this order? Is priesthood confined to *the* priesthood? Did the Church begin with priesthood or with *the* priesthood? Had the first Christians priests in the official sense, and did the Church spread outward and downward from them to an inferior grade of laymen? Or were the first Christians priests only in the universal sense, and did the priesthood arise from that as a ministry, as a mere matter of order, agency, and convenience? Is the priesthood a matter of *an* order, or of order merely? Is the whole Church historically an expansion from an official priesthood, or is an official ministry a projection of the universal priesthood, as an organism for a particular purpose throws out a limb? Was the existing ministry of the Church *devolved* from ministers appointed and endowed by Christ with unique powers and privileges, or was it *evolved*, in a historical way, by the Spirit-led Church itself, to meet the successive needs of the hour? These are questions which the Church must face and solve for its life. They are not academic, and not antiquarian. The great Christian issue of the hour turns on the conception of the Christian ministry. The brunt of the battle does not fall on the pews, but on the pulpit. It is not your place in the Church, but ours, that is in question. The issue put before you is not what place you claim for yourself in the Church, but what place you claim for your minister. As your minister, has he a place and right to his office in Christ equal to the officer of any Church in the world ? Is he as truly a servant of Christ's priesthood, and a waiter upon Christ's sacrifice, as those who stand by any altars in any Church ? If you truly understand your Christian place and duty as members of Christ and His Church, you assert for your ministry a right to minister Christ in all the fulness of His blessing, which is not exceeded by the ministry of any Church on earth, and your minister, as minister, meets every other on equal terms. That is your claim, the very meaning of your ecclesiastical existence as Free Churches. Make it courteously, but make it plainly ; and give it to be understood that when your minister makes that claim for his office, it is not his own claim he makes, but yours. If he is no true minister, then you are no true Church and no true Christians. The minister is what the Church is. He is a priest only in so far as he represents the essential priestliness inherent in the Church ; and the Church is priestly only in so far as it can represent the cross and sacrifice of Jesus Christ.

III

Is the priesthood and ministry of the Church a vicarious priesthood or a representative ? Christ's priesthood was vicarious. It did for man what he could never do for himself. It was not representative. It was not simply doing in a signal fashion what an ideal humanity does on the scale of the whole race. Of which nature is the priesthood in the Church? Does the minister of the Church do for the people with God what they cannot do for themselves? or does he only act on the Church's behalf, and fulfil conveniently a function which the Church really does through him? Is the priest chiefly and directly the organ of God to the Church, or the organ of the Church to God? Is he, then, to repeat the sacrifice of God, or to lead the sacrifice of man in Christ? Is he the dispenser of a sacrament or of a gospel? Is he a mediator or an instrument?

These are the questions to be met; and, in dealing with them, do not make the mistake of thinking that Protestantism stands for the universal priesthood alone, while Catholicism stands for an official priesthood alone. Even Roman Catholicism recognises a universal priesthood of all the faithful as well as Protestantism. Do not be puzzled if you hear a Catholic, while making exclusive claims for a sacerdotal order, insisting also on the priesthood of all believers. In the Catholic Catechism of the Council of Trent there is express mention made of the double priesthood. There is an inward and an outward. "All the faithful who are baptized are called priests. Especially so are those good men among them who have the Spirit of God, and by the kindness of God's grace are made living members of the High Priest Jesus Christ. Such men, by a faith inflamed with love, offer spiritual sacrifices to God on the altar of their souls; and to these sacrifices belong all good and honourable deeds which tend to the glory of God." " Thus," quotes the Catechism, " Christ made us a kingdom and priests to God and His Father by washing us in His own blood. We are a holy priesthood, offering spiritual sacrifices acceptable to God through Jesus Christ." All such texts refer to the inward priesthood. " But," the Catechism goes on to say, " The outward priesthood belongs not to all the faithful, but only to certain men, who are instituted and consecrated by the imposition of hands and the due rites of the Church to a specially sacred ministry. And the power of this outward priesthood is the power of offering to God the great sacrifice of the Church for the living and the dead— the Mass."

I have given you what is virtually a translation from the Latin of the Roman Catechism (ii. 7, 23). And I have done so that we may be quite fair to Catholicism, and may see that it does not deny a priesthood of all believers. The words in which it describes that priesthood are admirable; and they remind us well that the good and noble deeds of Christian men are more than noble and good—they are sacrificial and priestly acts offered to our spiritual God upon the altar of our soul. We have in our soul and self an altar whereto they have no access who merely serve the outward tabernacle of Humanity; and our Christian life is a most real priesthood. But we must recognise the following things in order also clearly to understand what our Protestantism means.

1. And, first, I ask you to notice that in this statement the priesthood of all believers is not theirs in virtue of their faith, but in virtue of their baptism. The faithful, even if devoted men, are called priests only after they have been baptized. The inward priesthood is constituted by the outward rite; and the outward rite is in the hands of the outward priesthood.

2. So that, after all, it is not the inward priesthood which is supreme in practice, but the outward. It is not faith that constitutes true priesthood, but only the faith of the baptized, faith which has been made possible by a rite, and which is at the mercy of that rite and of those who exercise it. The priest has a power over the believer, which is not given by the soul's spiritual faith. Faith is not its own justification. We are not justified by faith, but by faith which is made possible by a rite of the Church, an ordinance, a work

of the law. The spiritual value of faith is conditioned by a theurgic act in baptism; the higher gets its value from the lower, the inward from the outward, the moral from the magical. The clergy are the real mediators of the true priestly life, and in their priesthood the laity have no part. Moreover, that God may accept these good and noble acts of the lay soul, there is needed a *propitiatory* sacrifice, a sacrifice offered in the Mass, which is the privilege of the outward priesthood alone. And, further, that it may be *believers* who offer these lay sacrifices, their absolution is continually required, which absolution, again, is the function of the priest alone.

3. But the most serious remark on this distinction of the two priesthoods is this: It is not essential that those who have the powers of the outward priesthood should have the grace of the inward. The power of the outward priesthood is not derived from personal faith, love, or sacrifice, but from ordination, from the due institution by the hierarchy. The priest is not the holiest man, but the correctly appointed man; he is not the *truly* consecrated man, but only the *duly* consecrated. The virtue and validity of the sacraments are not affected, if it be afterwards found that the priest has been living in mortal sin. The most sacred and powerful position in the Church is not the holiest. Power and sanctity are disjoined. The

priesthood that gives the Church its priestly character is not the priesthood of sanctity, but only of function. This is Catholicism ; this comes of making the essence of the Church an institution instead of a Gospel, a rite instead of a faith.

The two priesthoods have, in fact, nothing in common except the name. They are not in essential and spiritual connection. The cleric is above the Church ; he becomes the Church ; he is described as a god. He draws his official power directly from God. He is the sole medium of grace for believers, who become and remain such only through the sacraments in his hands. And yet he need not be a personally holy man.

The evangelical position is a very clear antagonism. The spiritual office is a projection of the universal priesthood. It is an organ of the Church, and not Christ's vicar in the Church. The priestly character of the Church is not given *by* the priesthood, but *to* it. It has no mediatorial place, as the Church has but one mediator with God—Jesus Christ. It exercises no functions that do not belong by right to every Christian believer ; only for the sake of order it exercises them in a definite area. It is the faith of the Church that acts in the minister, and it may act through any member as minister for the time and occasion if the Church so will. The ministry is a mandate from the Church to act on its behalf and in its presence. The minister should not baptize where there are not enough present to make a small congregation ; nor should he administer the Lord's Supper to an invalid alone without two or three in the room. I bid you note particularly that the minister is the expression not of the individual's priesthood, but of the priesthood as universal, of the priesthood of the Church. It is the commission of the Church that he holds, not of individual faith, not of his own. If it were the latter, each member might claim the right to exhort and rebuke the whole Church, and pray in the whole Church, whether the Church asked him to do so or not. And that means an anarchy which ruined some of the Independent Churches of Scotland last century, which were not Churches at all, but groups of independent individuals. The minister is the mandatory of the priesthood of the whole Church, and not of isolated believers, not of his own faith alone. He must preach the Church's faith, even when his own is low, so long as it is not dead.

The Church conveys its rights and duties to the incumbent in trust, to exercise them on the whole Church's behalf amidst a particular community. He represents there the functions of the universal priesthood. What are they? The minister enters publicly the presence of God ; but that is every Christian's right as priest. He offers sacrifice, as it is every Christian's right to do, surrendering himself to God, body and soul, for the brethren, and bringing especially the fruit of the lips. The minister is the channel for others of God's grace in the Gospel; every Christian has the right and duty to be the like channel of the Gospel to his neighbours, whether he do it in word or in conduct, or in the special helpfulness of brotherly love to those who do not know how to claim their own rights to the same God. Christian philanthropy is a function of the universal priesthood. It is offering ourselves, our hearts and bodies, to Christ in His poor and His prodigals.

If you are a real Church, then, the call you give your minister puts him on the same footing as the minister of any Church whatever. The only difference between the different Protestant Churches in the matter is this: that for some, as the Anglicans, the Church is the whole historic body, with episcopal continuity through centuries, and bound by the ordinances of centuries; for others, as the Presbyterians, the Church is the existing community composed of a number of separate congregations; for others, like ourselves, it is the single local congregation of believers. According to these definitions, the mandate takes various shapes, and is less free or more. But they all differ from the idea of a ministry whose mandate is not *from* the

Church at all, but only *to* the Church, which is not in trust but in possession, which is not representative but vicarious.

There is a fine and clear passage of Luther on this head which I will quote :

"We take stand on this. There is no other word of God than that whose proclamation is enjoined on all Christians; there is no other baptism but that which any Christian may confer; there is no other memorial of the Lord's Supper but that which any Christian may make in obedience to Christ's command; there is no other sin than that which any Christian may bind or loose; there is no other sacrifice than the body [*i.e.* person] of any Christian. A Christian alone can truly pray, and Christians alone ought to judge of doctrine. And all these are royal and priestly things.

"Every Christian has the power which pope, bishop, priest, or monk has to retain sins or to remit. We have all that power. Only the stated and public exercise of it should be confined to those who are chosen for the purpose by the Church. But this does not affect its private use.

"Every Christian has the true clerical status. There is no difference among them, except as a matter of order."

And the Smalcaldic Articles say : "If the bishops

became the enemies of the Church, and refused to ordain proper persons, the Churches could take back their rights. For where the Church is, there is the right to administer the Gospel. It belongs to the Church, and no human power can take it from the Church."

IV

But our chief interest in this country is not with the Roman idea of the priesthood, but with the Anglican, and its relation to our own ministry. What is the Anglican idea of the ministry of the Church? I leave out of account those extremists in it who really take the Roman view; and I would go to those quarters where the High Anglican view is expressly put, in contrast with Rome on the one hand, and the Puritans on the other; to the Oxford High Churchism of Canon Gore and Dr. Moberly, as distinct from the Cambridge Broad Churchism of Bishop Lightfoot on this point.

It clears the ground by repudiating the Roman idea of the priest as the basis of the Church, and by himself the Church; it discards the vicarious view of the priesthood; and it starts from the principle, not of a sacerdotal order, but of a sacerdotal Church. It is the Church that is the priestly body—the whole Church, lay and cleric, as one spiritual unity. It believes in

the universal priesthood of the Church ; not so much
the priesthood of every individual by himself, but the
priesthood of a collective Church, in which all individuals are on the same spiritual footing. This
Church needs officers and organs to give effect to its
priestly quality. It needs representatives through
whom it may act. These are its priests, strictly so
called. They *are* representative. They do draw
their authority from the universal priesthood of the
whole Church ; they do not draw their authority
direct from God, and impose it on the Church. They
do not confer on the Church its priestliness ; they
only express and represent it. It is a representative
and not a vicarious priesthood. It is appointed by the
whole Church. But then it is not *directly* appointed
by the whole Church, not elected. It is appointed by
the due authority in the Church. The *sacerdotal* authority is ideally a mandate from the Church, an exercise
of the Church's own priestliness, but it is conferred by
the *governmental* authority of the Church. Now what
is this governmental authority of the Church which
has the sole right to appoint the Church's ministers as
vehicles of the Church's inherent priestliness ? It is
the episcopate. The episcopate has, from the beginning, been the only legitimate organ of the authority
of the whole Church. The bishops represent the
Church, and they rule it only because they do repre-

sent it. Their power is constitutional, as becomes Englishmen, and not despotic, like Rome's. But how came the episcopate by this sole power for the Church of Christ? They received it directly from the apostles. And the apostles? They had it conferred on them by direct commission from Christ. Christ appointed His apostles, but He appointed them not as satraps, but as representatives of the whole Church; they were to concentrate and exercise the spiritual power which He really conveyed to the whole Church. Moreover, it is said, He gave them power to convey their commission and authority to the bishops; and the bishops, as the sole organs and administrators of the Church's spiritual prerogative, had the sole right of appointing the Church's ministers. You will remember that the minister, then, on the true Anglican theory, represents the Church, and does not rule it; that his priestliness is only the personalized expression of the priestliness of the whole Church, lay and cleric together; that he has nothing which the whole Church does not convey to him out of its own nature and prerogative as priestly through Christ in the world and for it.

V

Now if we concede the inherent priesthood of the whole Church everywhere (as we must), what is there to be said in criticism of this position? Why do we object to it?

Is it not clear, to begin, that our first point of issue (granted that concession) is not so much with the priest as with the authority that claims to monopolize for the whole Christian Church the right to appoint him, viz. the episcopate? Both we and they, of course, are eager to know and do the will of Christ in the matter, and we both recognise the supreme priestliness of the Church under Christ. Was it the will and commission of Christ that the episcopate alone should have the sole right to appoint the ministry of the Church, to institute the organs of its priestliness; that the bishops should inherit the prerogative of the apostles? That is a very large question. It turns on the interpretation of Scripture; and opposite views are held about it by scholars of the Oxford school, and by the great New Testament scholars of the Cambridge school. But it is well that we should not allow any indignation with the Romanizing priests of the Anglican Church to blind us to the real location of the issue in that Church's most responsible speakers. The real conflict is on the episcopal monopoly of appointing officers, who are yet not officers of the hierarchy, as in Rome, but, like our own ministers, representative officers of the Church, though they can be ordained only by the ministry. Can the real representatives of the Church's priestliness be appointed by authority? An occasional and rare representative may be appointed by authority—as an ambassador; but can the standing representation of the Church's ultimate and characteristic power be an appointed one, and remain representative in any real and effectual sense? I venture to think it cannot. I venture to think that the doctrine of the apostolic succession is incompatible with a truly representative priesthood, and in practice destroys its representative quality, and tends to turn it into the Romish and vicarious thing. I think this is shown by two features in the Anglican clergy: first, by the relation which a vast and increasing number of them take up to their own flock —shown in sympathy with the mass and the confessional; second, by the unhappy attitude and tone taken to the ministers of other Churches.

VI

But as a theory the Anglican is really very different from the Roman, because it does make the priest the representative and projection of the priestliness of the whole Church. But it is not the New Testament theory. And, as I say, I fear that practically and popularly it is not easily distinguishable from the Roman theory; and it is constantly passing over into it.

And the reasons are these:

1. The representative nature of the priesthood is too remote from the Church's own priestly sense at a given time for the Church to feel represented.

(*a*) The bishop who gives the minister his validity in the first place is not appointed by the Church, but by the government of the day—by the premier of the day. This really takes the authorization of the ministry entirely out of the hands of the believing and priestly Church, and has long broken the true succession; for it can hardly be said that most premiers or most monarchs represent the Church either in its faith or in its priestly quality.

(*b*) Even where the bishops are elected by the Church it is by the clergy, *i.e.* by those whom bishops had appointed, and therefore not by any electors representing the lay priestliness, the *sacerdotium laici*, in the Church. It really works in a circle —bishops appointing priests, and priests appointing bishops—which makes the ministry a close body outside of the universal priestliness of the Church.

(*c*) For the chief authority of the episcopate we are referred to the apostles and appointment by them. But their procedure is very obscure. We are without information as to any principles of representation followed by the apostles in their selection. The gap in their own college they filled up by lottery. And it carries us a very long way round from the priestly quality of the living Church to-day to seek its recognition, and expression, and only valid authority in the apostles of two thousand years ago ; an authority, too, based on a commission given before Pentecost, before there was a Church, a commission which they understood in no sense which forbade the use of the lottery. Even if they represented the priestliness of the then Church, it places the priestliness of to-day's Church at a great disadvantage, and even reduces it to an insignificant point, if the representatives to-day have to go back so far for their authority to represent it.

2. But what we are told is that the representative authority of the apostles was theirs as appointed by Christ, and that in travelling back to them with the ministry we are going back to an ordination which is divine in the first degree ; they represent the Church, not by the representative principle, but by Christ's will that they should. Well, but if that be so, have we in any real sense the representative character of the ministry, as the expression of the Church's priestliness ? The priesthood *then* does not flow out of the universal priesthood of the Church conferred by an indwelling Christ, but is parallel with it. Both priesthoods are the gift of Christ, and the one is not the representative of the other. If the Church appointed its priests, they *might* be representative. But can they represent, can they flow from, the Church's priestly quality, can

they do more than illustrate it, if they owe their appointments even to the personal institution of Christ on earth, and not to His indwelling Spirit acting through the Church? Even if Christ appointed the apostles to represent an infant Church which was not yet sufficiently knit or adult to appoint its own representatives, where did He tell them to keep the Church continually in this state of minority? where did He empower them to monopolize from the Church *in which He dwelt* the continuous appointment of their successors? The theory of an apostolic succession is incompatible with the faith of a Church made priestly by the indwelling Spirit of the great High Priest. The right of the ministry is due, we are told, to its being an expression and representation of the priestliness of the Church. The Church conveys and confers this priestliness through the authority of the bishop. But the authority of the bishop is not held to be derived from the Church, but directly from the same power to which the Church owes its priestliness, viz. Christ Himself. Therefore what the bishop conveys in ordination is not the priestliness of the Church, but a priestly character conveyed to the episcopate through the apostles over the head of the Church and direct from Christ Himself. And so we reach Rome.

Can we wonder if this is practically indistinguishable from the Roman theory in its results? Can we wonder if the Church has very little sense of its own priestliness compared with that of the priestly order, when the modern representative principle is overruled by miraculous institution and ancient prerogative, and when so many centuries and so many intermediaries are placed between its intrinsic priestliness and the priestliness of its representative staff? The living Church, whose priestly quality is said to be represented by its minister, has no real voice or action in connection with his appointment. Can we wonder if it do not *feel* represented, if it never think of the representative theory in connection with its ministry, and if it look upon any sanctity it may itself possess as devolved from the priest rather than upon the priest as evolved from its native sanctity and priesthood in Christ? A devolved ministry is incompatible with a representative ministry unless the authority which devolves is placed there by direct election by the living Church. If the Church do not elect its minister, it should at least elect the bishops who appoint the minister.

The defect of the Anglican theory, therefore, is a practical more than a theoretical one. Its theory is so embarrassed and so worked as to produce a practical result fatal to the theory. It does not give practical effect to the Church's universal priesthood. It does not make the Church feel that priesthood by comparison with the specific priesthood. It creates a wrong emphasis, the tendency of which is constantly to turn the representative priesthood into a vicarious, and lose the sacerdotal Church in the independent priesthood of the successors of the apostles.

3. But there is another and more serious reason why this Anglican theory of the ministry tends to pass over into the Roman, and its priesthood to gravitate to the Mass. We are told by one of its finest and most responsible exponents (Dr. Moberly) that the theory is really twofold. First, the priest is what the Church is; second, the Church is what Christ is. First, the priest represents the priestly Church. "The priesthood of the ministry is the priesthood of the Church specialized and personified in certain representative instruments." The priest is what the Church is in this respect. He cannot rise higher than his source and reservoir, which is the priestliness of the whole Church. That seems to shut out the Roman theory of a commissioned vicar of Christ, and confine us to the view of the priest as an organ of the Church. But I have just shown how the practical application of the principle tends to neutralize it. I come now to the next step taken, the definition of the Church's own priestliness, which does not arrest that tendency Romeward, but helps it. For the priestliness of the Church is defined thus: "What Christ is the Church must be." " Christ is the spirit and

principle of divine love and sacrifice in the conditions of human sin. He is that principle incarnate. This the Church must be by His indwelling, and by her self-identification with Him." Well, that is sound and fine. But there is an action of Christ's sacrifice which goes beyond these words; there is its action upon God and the holiness of God, as well as its expression of the love and sacrifice of God. There is the atoning action and aspect of Christ's sacrifice. Does the Church, by any self-identification with the sacrifice of Christ, share that in an active way? In a passive way, yes; the Church enjoys the benefits and blessings of that atoning sacrifice. But does the Church share that act, the eternal atoning act? Is its sacrifice in any sense propitiatory? Is its priesthood a share of *this* part of Christ's priesthood? The Church may offer, must offer, Christ and the sacrifice made by Christ. Indeed in the Church's offerings Christ indwelling offers Himself afresh. And in heaven He offers perpetually to God His atoning sacrifice. But, in offering Himself through the act of the Church by His indwelling and inspiration, is it the atoning effect of His sacrifice that He offers? Is it in any sense an atoning sacrifice that the Church offers, even when it gives full effect to the reality of its priesthood in Him? If it is, are we not landed in the bosom of Rome, with its sacrifice of the Mass *vere propitiatorium*? We need not hesitate to say that the priestliness in the Church is a sacrificing priestliness, but is it an atoning? The Church shares Christ's sacrifice of love, identifies herself with it; does she share His sacrifice of grace? She identifies herself with Him in act as a sacrifice for the *blessing* of the world; can she identify herself with Him as a sacrifice for the *saving* of the world? She identifies herself with her Redeemer; yes, but *as* Redeemer? as the Redeemer of the world? Does she share in the act of redeeming, as she does in the act of reconciling men?

I shall have something to say presently to indicate that the Church's function as the *Body* of Christ is not complete; by this metaphor alone we might even construe the Church in terms of a certain Christian pantheism; and it needs to be supplemented by the more fundamental conception of the Church as the *Bride* of Christ, as the object of His grace before she is the organ of His action in men, as a respondent before she is an agent, as a will confronting His before she is a will effecting His. And what makes the Church His Bride is the atoning, redeeming act which took her out of the world, an act which she does not share but only answers. If the priestliness of the Church mean a share, even a conferred share, of the atoning act, if she reproduce not only Christ's sacrifice but also His atonement, His Redemption, then it is hard to see how we are to avoid the Roman theory of the Church as a prolongation of the Incarnation, and the priest as a demigod. It is a theory with a speculative fascination. The chief fascination of Rome to-day *is* speculative and imaginative. But it is a theory with all the immense practical results that Rome's masterly logic (given her principles) can draw.

But is the Anglican theory exposed to any such risk? Does it claim for the priestliness of the Church a share in the atoning aspect and effect of Christian sacrifice? Well says Dr. Moberly (I grieve to take a controversial attitude to a book so true, profound, and beautiful in many respects as his *Ministerial Priesthood*), "What Christ is the Church must be. She is priestly in the Eucharist, which is her ceremonial identification with the atoning sacrifice." " The priesthood of Christ is His offering of Himself as a perfect sacrifice, an offering which is not more an outward enactment than an inward perfecting of holiness and of love; an offering whose outward enactment is but the perfect utterance of a perfect inwardness; an offering which, whilst, so to say, containing Calvary in itself, is consummated eternally by His eternal self-presentation before the presence and on the throne of God. The sacrificial priesthood of the Church is really her identification with the priesthood and sacrifice of Christ." " Christ Himself has presented for all time an outward ceremonial, which is the symbolic counterpart in the Church on earth, not simply of Calvary, but of that eternal presentation of Himself in heaven in which Calvary is vitally contained. Through this symbolic enactment, rightly understood—an enactment founded on, and intrinsically implying, as well as recalling, Calvary —she in her Eucharistic worship on earth is identified with His sacrificial self-oblation to the Father; she is transfigured up into the scene of the unceasing commemoration of His sacrifice in heaven, or the scene of His eternal offering in heaven is translated down to, and presented, and realized in the worship on earth."

How much in this is admirable, but how much is inadequate! The writer does not seem to me to grasp with evangelical depth and fulness the essence of the redeeming act; he does not touch the main trunk of the evangelical nerve. The action of Christ is regarded too exclusively as a manifestation and presentation of holiness, *i.e.* too æsthetically, and too little as an act of will, a great act of struggle and conquest, a great transaction of some sort dealing with the divine and holy law. It is too apodeictic and too little pragmatic. If the atonement was no more than Christ's sacrificial self-presentation to the Father, if His holiness was not in its nature a unitary and compendious holy *act* pervading His life earthly and heavenly, if it was the world-conflict with evil and its conquest; then the Church may be identified with it. But if it was this last, if it had an absolute value in regard to broken law and objective holiness, if there was thus a winepress which He trod and treads alone, and of the people there can be none with Him, then the account above given falls short; and falls short in the very point which is the focus of redeeming action. And there is in the atoning sacrifice and priesthood that which the priestliness of the Church can never share, that which Catholicism fails to realize, and which, when realized, is the evangelical fulcrum of the Reformation that displaced Catholicism from the throne of the Church.

The Catholic theory may be profound as it is certainly acute, but it is not the profoundest; and it does not keep pace with the searching of the Spirit in the mighty men of the Reformation. It is a theory more scholarly than profound, and more beautiful than powerful. But the point I would press here is this, that while its lack of profundity commends it with charm to many, its lack of searching precision renders it a too easy prey to Roman logic. And we cannot wonder if, when the Eucharist is described as the Church's identification with the Atoning Sacrifice and the priest is held to be what the Church is, such a theory of priestly function should be indistinguishable from the Mass except to trained and ingenious minds.

VII

But with the reserve I name, I should like to insist that the true nature of the Church is priestly, that the Church is the priest in the kingdom of God, and that the minister of the Church represents that priestliness. It is a priestliness which belongs to every member of the Church, not as an isolated unit, but as a member organized through faith into the priestliness of Christ. To be a priest is the power, right, and privilege of every member of the Christian Church in so far as it is a Church of believers. It is not the power or right of one who is a member of the Church only by tradition, habit, baptism, or ordination. What makes a priest is personal faith in the great High Priest. It is not the power or right of any one who is a member of the Church just because he is a member of the State whose national Church it is. Justification by faith is ordination to the true priesthood. But when we come to the public and official ministry, what Anglicanism says and Presbyterianism says is true. There should be a conveyance by the Church to the person concerned of whatever its priestly function may mean in a public way. The private Christian shares the Church's priestly power and right of access to God; but when it is a question of *authority* to speak and act in the Church's name, and to do so habitually, then the authority should come from the Church by express institution. That is our own congregational principle. Any believing man has the right and power to speak the Gospel to any men he may get to listen. But if he is to speak and act on behalf of the Church, if he is to represent the Gospel community, he must be appointed thereto by the community.

They may appoint him for a particular occasion only, and ask him to address them, pray for them, act for them in a public way, only *ad hoc*, as we do in our prayer meetings. In so doing, in so praying especially, the member of the Church becomes for the time a minister of the Church, yea, a priest, leading the Church's sacrifice of prayer at the spiritual altar, and giving outward effect to the inner priesthood of the Church. No man taketh this honour unto himself, but those alone who are invited to do so by the Church, if only through the request of its presiding and permanent minister in the chair. If each claim the authority to act for the Church on his own impulse and initiative, then we have anarchy.

Or the minister of the Church may be appointed by it for life, for standing office. He is then the permanent and personal representative of the priestly Church; but he is so only by the direct appointment of the Church. He is a true representative of it by the voice of the Spirit in its election. He receives authority, not to preach the Gospel but to represent the Church. There is not added to him any spiritual power that he did not possess before, or any Christian grace; but he has authority to speak in the Church's name as he could not before. He can speak as the organ of a community, and so act. Priestly he is, and not merely a prophet; but he is only a priest in the sense that he represents the priestly function of the collective Church within the world. As a member of the Church he had power and right before; what he receives for the Church is authority as a matter of convenience and order alone. And he has it from the Church directly, not by a circuit of centuries, nor by a bishop who is a creation of the State more than the Church. His election by the faithful communicants makes him a minister of the universal Church and the representative of whatever priestliness belongs to that.

You will see that my remarks in these discourses are not merely a criticism of another Church system, but also a protest against a tone which has crept into our own. The very murmurs with which some may receive this plea for the priestly nature, the sacerdotal function, of the Church in the world and for it—these demurrers show that the preacher on this line has some duty to expand the attenuation of the Church among his own no less than to assail the exaggerations of it in others.

IV.—Part II

SOME REAL SOURCES OF THE PRIEST'S WELCOME

I

A PRIESTLY order cannot be turned to safe account by anything but a more priestly Church. The State cannot do it, the world cannot; because, after all, its idea is much higher than any belonging to the mere natural man. Even a Church, if devoid of a real sense of its priestliness, will be unable to cope with the priest who takes the priesthood in earnest, in however perverted a form. I may therefore, perhaps, be forgiven if I repeat or dwell on this article of a priestly Church in the interest of our Evangelical faith and the reality of our Church life.

The priesthood which the ministry represents is the priesthood of the Church rather than of isolated believers. This Church where I preside is a priest much more than I am, more than any member of it is, more than any clergyman. The great visible priest on earth is the Church in its various sections.

The Church is the great *intermediary* between God and man, because it is in trust of the one saving Gospel of the Great *Mediator*. The Church is the priest as the abode and agent on earth of the One Priest, the High Priest. It is priest by its unction of the Holy Ghost. The minister of the Church only represents the Church's priesthood, which conveys a great function of Christ's. The Church is primary, the office secondary. The ministry is not an order, but an office. The priest is what the Church is; it is not the Church that is what the priest is. The Church is the steward of the Gospel; and the priest's authority is only the authority of the Gospel committed to him. The sacraments in the minister's hands are only there because he himself is the hand of the Church; and they draw their value from the Word of the Church's Gospel of the One High Priest. They are expressions of it; and therefore they are in their nature not magical, but moral and spiritual as the effect of the Gospel is. The minister is in charge of the sacraments just as he is of the Gospel, which is the common charge of the Church.

We cannot be brought to like the word priest for the minister of the Church. It was avoided in the New Testament, I have said, because it had become associated with ideas foreign to Christian office. And if that was the case then, it is equally the case now.

The word through its Roman use has become so hopelessly debased that it is mischievous to retain it. And the Anglican Church puts itself into a false position with the public by the attempt to do so. But, for all that, there is nothing that some of the Free Churches need more than a return to the idea of the priestly character of the Church, of the collective Church, whatever we may regard as its unit. That unit may be the Episcopal Church, or the Presbyterian, or the single local Church; yet if it is a real Church of Christ it is a priestly body in its nature and function in the world. The reason why we are not in earnest enough, and our piety is of a poor, flat, and unimpressive type, making too little appeal to the public soul and imagination, is because we have lost the idea that our Church is, in its nature, as the body of Christ, a priest among men. Our individualism has lost the sense of the Church as a real body; it is regarded as an association of people each having his own personal relations with God. And our secularity of mind has lost the idea of the Church as a priestly body exercising under Christ the great sacrificial function of the world. The name of priest, which we would refuse to the Church's minister, we should urge for the Church itself, for the sake of the thing it represents. The main business of the Church on earth is priestly; it is to show forth, so far as the redeemed may do, the Redeemer's death in His risen light and power.

Is it enough to describe the Church simply as a witness to the world of Christ's truth, as declaring to the world reconciliation and redemption? Is the Church simply a messenger from Christ to men? Does not Christ do more than send it? Does He not dwell in it? Does He not act from the midst of it? Is it not His chief and chosen organ on earth? And is not His great action based on the perpetual sacrifice of Himself for the world? Must the Church He inhabits and uses not become in some sense the organ on earth of that action? Does the Church not offer sacrifice as well as proclaim truth? Does she not offer Christ Himself to men? does she not plead Christ for men before God? Is not the great sacrifice Christ, both to God and to man? and does the Church not offer this spiritual sacrifice in manifold ways continually?

We might begin with our questions lower in the spiritual scale. We might ask, is not the whole sphere of Christian action a spiritual sacrifice? We present our bodily energies in duty or service, as a living and sacred sacrifice. If the Church sacrifice itself at all in the service of man, it is a priestly act. But we rise higher. When the Church does that is it showing forth its own affection for men? No. It is setting forth the love of God to men in action—

not in word, but in deed. But that is what the sacrifice of Christ did. It is the sacrifice of Christ living on and working itself out through the Church. It is the Church doing the priestly act of expressing the priesthood of Christ in one aspect of it at least. But the Church does still more. It not only shows in service the love that made Christ die, but it carries home through this loving service the fact of the Reconciliation. Its service of man is not merely to help man, but to reveal God, to reveal by this help, the Redeemer, the cross. Its work and service for man is not only sacrificial but sacramental, both for its members and for the world. By its loving service it does more than show forth, it conveys. It is a channel and agent of grace from Christ to man. It is a standing sacrament, a priestly minister. It administers by its sacrifice the Great Sacrifice. And if we turn from its work to its word, is its word a mere word, a mere declaration, such as a herald might read out at a market cross, or the *Gazette* publish in the King's name? The preached word of the Gospel—is it not more than the delivery of a report, is it not a work itself? When I preach a sermon am I reading a paper, an essay, an information? Am I getting out a fine composition, publishing a theory, giving a lecture, explaining a piece of the moral world, airing views and opinions? Am I speaking to critics or to believers? There is indeed not enough criticism of the right kind. There is criticism of some phrase or manner when it should be the ideas. But it is not to criticism that the preacher speaks chiefly, but to faith, to believers, to critics on their believing side, to what they and he have in common, to their Christian need, sympathy and hope. Take the greatest preacher and the truest—what is he trying to do? To exhibit himself, to sparkle, to please, to instruct agreeably, to win popular influence for God? Does he want to send men away saying "How well he has done!" instead of "How well *we* must do!"? No; the word of the Gospel preached, like every divine word, is a work, it is a spiritual act. Why is the preacher exhausted as the lecturer is not? Because it is a spiritual struggle, the Lord's controversy. He has been wrestling with men—at grips with their soul, their fugitive, reluctant, recalcitrant soul. Because every best sermon is a real spiritual act, an act of the Church moreover, of the Church which is God's channel and agent of grace and prayer for men, of the priestly Church. Every great true sermon is a great true sacrament, the sacrament of the word, in which the people participate as really as the preacher. It is not his message, but the Church's. It is faith preaching. The Church delivers itself through him. Every true hearer is not a hearer only, but a doer of the word. To hear well is to do something actively, to do much. To hear as the Church should hear is really to preach. The preacher is but the mouthpiece of the Church, with its Gospel of the great saving act. In every real Gospel sermon God gives the word and great is the company of the preachers. On every such occasion those who hear in faith are not simply present, do not simply listen, they assist in the service. They exercise their universal priesthood. They minister at the altar of the word of the cross. If that were realised it would put a new aspect upon church-going. Men would go there in the same spirit as the minister goes, and to do the same work in their way. They would go to something in which they were not passive but active, not a mere audience but colleagues in the ministry, and deacons serving the tables of the word. The pulpit of the true Gospel is itself an altar where the eternal sacrifice is offered through men by Christ the High Priest to men, and by men in a Church of praying priests to God. In the preaching of the word of the cross the Church is a priestly Church. It is really the Church that preaches, and for the Church to preach Christ in His eternal sacrifice is for the Church to offer that sacrifice in the only sense in which men can offer a sacrifice provided, yea, made by God.

But we go higher still in a way. The Church not

only helps and serves men in the love of Christ, not only bears home the Gospel in a sacrificing, sacramental way, by act or by word, but the Church prays for men. And this is perhaps the priestliest function of all. The Church identifies itself with the perpetual intercession of our Eternal High Priest. The Church through Christ has access to God on man's behalf. In true prayer the Church is priestly in two ways. It is solid with man, for whom it offers intercession ; and it is solid with the perpetual intercession of Christ, offered for Church and world alike. This is the greatest act of philanthropy that the Church can do, and at present the most neglected by many. I need only mention here, as I have come to the worship and prayer of the Church, the supreme act of worship in the Lord's Supper. In that act the Church identifies itself, within the limits I have said, in a ceremonial way with Christ in His sacrificial act. It offers Christ, the one eternal sacrifice, to God. And Christ dwelling in His Church body offers Himself, preaches Himself to the world as crucified Redeemer, in an act of a different nature from the spoken act of the pulpit. All these considerations make the function of the Church not only the prophet's, but the priest's. They make the Church in some sense under Christ not only the apostle of reconciliation, but also a reconciler.

II

The Church is in some sense reconciling, mediating, and priestly. In what sense? It must be in a sense prescribed by the nature of Christ's priesthood, because that is what constituted the Church. Its function is determined by the priestly act and nature of its indwelling Christ. What is the relation of the Church's mediation, the Church's intercession, to Christ's? It can never, of course, be parallel or mediatorial, as if anything offered by the Church were in itself a true, real, and proper sacrifice, a *verum et proprium sacrificium*, with a propitiatory value of its own. It cannot be *vere propitiatorium*, as the Roman Catechism says of its mass. The action of a body which owes its existence and nature to another continuous and constitutive act can never be its parallel. The Church's action can never be a repetition of Christ's redemption or intercession, nor can it be a mere imitation of His teaching, healing, and blessing of man. It cannot approach His act from the outside. It can only be a function of that act within us; it can only be the reproduction of that act working itself out in the Church. It is in us and through us rather than by us. If the Church be the medium of God's forgiveness to the world, it is only as the organ of the One Mediator. She does not produce the forgiveness, but only reproduces it. But she does reproduce it, she does not only declare it. She gives it actual practical effect. She carries it home effectually and sacramentally to men's experience. The Church cannot forgive—only her Lord can do that—but I do not think, if we had the proper views of the ministry, that it would be dangerous to say that the Church absolves. It cannot destroy guilt—God alone can do that in Christ—but it could, if it were its true, kind, holy self toward the poor soul, destroy the difficulty of believing that God had done so. It could destroy the sinner's difficulty in taking forgiveness in earnest. The priestly Church is yet not so priestly that it can expiate, propitiate, atone; but it can offer God's own expiation both to God and man, and it can do so not in an external way, but by an identification of itself with that expiation, Christ. The only propitiation it offers is Christ, who is the foregone offering from God Himself. The Church cannot atone, but it can and does offer His atonement who could and did. It bears into God's sight, so to say, the foregone propitiation, the Lamb that God has provided for an offering. It offers this to God in a sacrifice of its self-righteousness and self-will. And it offers also to men. It offers to men this sacrifice and atonement of Christ. It sets Him forth as their propitiation. It offers it in word, in rite, and in the humane and loving ministries in which our faith grows sacramental to our kind. The priestly sacrifices of the Church are only representative, and not vicarious. But they represent in act, not in show. They effect, and not only declare. They "exhibit," in the old and pregnant sense of the word. They represent, by reproducing it, the manward side of the sacrifice of Christ. They also represent and embody the sacrifices of man in grateful response to Christ's. But they are not instead of either God's sacrifices or man's, they are rather expressive and prophetic of these. These act through them. No priestly function of the Church adds anything to what Christ has done; it only explicates His act, actualises it variously in history and life. But it does explicate it. It does not merely either commemorate or imitate it. It is an act within His universal act, it is not an act contributed to it.

The priestly character of the Church therefore rests on the indwelling in it of its own Priest and Redeemer. It rests on a share which the Church thus has, as a conscious and obedient organ, in His perpetual priestly work. But that priestly work is twofold—it is sacrificial, and it is atoning. It blesses through loving self-surrender, and it satisfies a holy broken law. Now in this latter function of Christ the Church does not share. There she is not the Body of Christ, but the Bride of Christ; not the organ of His sacrificing love, nor the channel of His gospel of grace, but the recipient of His grace, the respondent to it, the heart that is made what it is by it. The error of Rome is to exalt the idea of the Church as Christ's Body at the cost of the idea of the Church as His Bride. It claims a share too intimate and organic in the priestly work of Christ on its atoning side. His grace is too much a thing infused into it, and too little a thing exercised towards it. The believing Church is such because of its practical belief in Christ's atoning work. It is this faith that forms its priesthood. But the object of faith must be something which confronts us even more than something we share. Therefore we cannot share the atoning work that we trust, but its benefits only. These we do share, and among them chiefly the spirit of sacrifice and the work of reconciling men. Our priesthood is a priesthood of the Reconciliation, not of the Redemption; of the attuning of men rather than of the atoning of God. But our reconciling sacrifices must rest on the atoning sacrifice, otherwise the priesthood of believers is a metaphor and a theme more than a principle.

III

A priestly order can only be safely used by a more priestly Church. But how is the real priestliness of the Church to be found and fed? Only by the Church's return to a personal acquaintance both intellectual and spiritual with the New Testament.

We cannot settle this strife by any knowledge of the second or third century. That would leave its settlement in the hands of the scholars, not to say the archæologists. We must go to the first century, and take the scholars with us as our assessors and advisers there. The English Christian public must become much better acquainted with the Bible if we are to be saved from the priest for the true priesthood. Without the Bible the public is powerless against the priest; with the Bible the priest becomes the Church's servant and minister for the public. It is the Bible that must both restore us to the Church and protect us from the Church. It was given for that purpose. It was not the product of the Church. That is a fallacy of which sections of the Church make great use. The Church gave us the canon, but it did not give us the books. Holy men moved by the spirit were the authors of these. The Church is the librarian more than the author. It selected the books and it preserved them. It has also acted as interpreter, but without finality. It is more correct to regard the Bible and the Church as parallel products of the Spirit, than to treat the Church as producing the Bible, and therefore in sole possession of the right of interpretation. In the Bible resides a power to reform the Church, far higher than any power in the Church to reconstruct the Bible. The scholarship of the Church may reconstruct the Bible, but it has no power to reconstruct the Gospel in the Bible; and that Gospel has the power to reconstruct both Bible and Church, and especially to save us from the Church's perversions and corruptions of its own priestly power.

The Free Churches must, one way or another, read and understand more of the Bible. All their worst misfortunes, difficulties, and inadequacies have arisen by the practical dropping of the Bible from their personal acquaintance and use. It has been squeezed out by other literature, much of it religious. The new art of printing gave the Bible at the Reformation into the hands of the Christian public, but to-day it is the art of printing that has thrust it out of their hands. It is the immense accessible mass of printed matter comparatively worthless that has preoccupied the reading time of most Christian people, till their religious taste and intelligence is of the lightest kind. There ought to be a system of daily Bible reading at work in every Church. We have Home Reading Unions of the most useful kind for other literature, and there ought to be in the Churches something of the kind for the Bible. Let the Christian public only become quite sure that the vicarious priest (in theory or in effect) is foreign to the New Testament, and there is enough of the Protestant principle left as to the authority of Scripture to send him back to his native Rome, or confine him to a small and harmless sect.

For a personal and intelligent use of the New Testament means personal and experiential faith, personal and open-eyed religion. And it is such personal religion that is the essence of Christianity. It is the fact that the priest is a religious person who knows his own narrow mind that gives him so much of his effect. Men will always trust a lucid and living person more than either a system or a book. The true priestliness of the Church is an abstraction if it do not work through living, convinced, and priestly persons. They may be official or they may be spiritual, but either way they go for more than a system and an abstraction. And we can only overcome a mere official priesthood by a priestliness in ourselves more deeply personal, just as in philosophy we overcome rationalism by a deeper reasonableness. It is the personal effect that we give to the faith of our own priestliness in Christ that is its real power with men. We must love them for His sake, help and serve them, live the Gospel into them, intercede for them, and be a refuge to them which they do not find in worldlings like themselves. We must exercise the priesthood of faith and character, of faith and conduct, of faith and love, of faith and mercy. The Spirit's action is through spiritual men. We must live into earth the perpetual priesthood of Christ in heaven; we must *become* sacraments to men, and not merely use them. We must be the sacrifices we preach—be, like our Lord, in some guarded sense, at once priest and victim, offering ourselves in the priestly communion of a Church of blessed martyrs. For the priestly malady is too deep and subtle to be cured by anything but a priestly life in the true principle and power of the real active presence in us by faith of the High Priest of our profession, Jesus Christ. The sanctity of the priest can only be met and mended by the instructed holiness of the truly redeemed. The fountain of the true priesthood is not the bishop, nor even the institution of Christ, but the cross of Christ and its action on our personal sin and faith. The one power which the priest has to dread is the power of men certainly forgiven without him—broken by Christ and by Christ restored, bruised and healed by the same Saviour—men who, being justified by faith without works or priests of a law, have peace and power with God as priests indeed through Jesus Christ.

IV

I have indicated those ennobling aspects of the high sacerdotal view which give it such footing as it has in the true priestly idea of faith and of the Church. And I should like to admit my belief that much of what seems the extravagance of the priesthood is due (like total abstinence in its direction) to a spiritual sense of the need for an extreme protest against, on the one hand, the passionate worldliness, luxury, and vulgarity of a wealthy and secular age, and, on the other, the irreverence and familiarity of a type of religion either too sentimental or too hard. But there are sides also in which the priesthood appeals to less spiritual instincts, and finds a soil in the very ordinary man. One of the features of the present day which imperils the Protestant position is a popular debasement of the sound tendency to think of the essence of religion as doing something; from which it is a ready step to think that the essential sacrifice is an act in the outward and usual sense of a deed—a *gestum* instead of an *actum*. Practical religion becomes a religion of performances and achievements instead of experiences and spiritual acts. A sacrament comes to take its value from being an *opus operatum* instead of a phase of the great decisive spiritual act spread through the life—the act of faith. This is the soul of sacrifice, the supreme sacrificial act; it is the act of self-surrender, of self-committal in faith. This is the act which constitutes Christian priesthood. This is the central oblation offered by the Christian man. It is the community of this act of faith that is the universal priesthood of the Church. Every outward act is an expression and a detail of this act, into which is put the whole energy of the Christian soul. It is true, so far, that faith is doing something, though not in the popular sense. Religion is an act, and a sacrificial act; but it is an act of the inward soul, a continuous act of life-trust, in which the ethical rises to the spiritual while it remains of the will. The ethical becomes spiritual because its object is a person, not a law. It is the soul's act of self-committal to the sacrifice of Christ. It is personal faith in a personal Redeemer. But it is untrue to say that religion is an act in the sense that it is either conduct or sacraments. The priesthood of the Christian must be effective in something else before it take form in either of these. It is his personal relation of total surrender to the priesthood of Christ.

Now it is the popular idea of the average man (to whom Christ never made His appeal), the idea of religion as some form of action rather than a spiritual quality of act—it is this idea that makes the work of the vicarious and operating priest so congenial to many minds in an energetic age and race. "I like men who do things," says a somewhat mannish girl in one of Mr. Kipling's stories. And there is a mannish quality about the God of the period,[1] about the religious object of the average Briton, which is sufficiently expressed in these words. His idea of faith is not an act and committal of the soul once for all, but a series of self-devotions. The popular hero is a person of exploits without a spiritual interior. Religion comes to mean doing certain things; and it is not doing the one hidden thing needful and eternal, by which the soul gives priestly value to all the things it essays. There is an obviousness about the priest's spectacular act at the altar which commends it much to this habit of mind. In this respect the mass is simply the ritual counterpart of the ethical tendency in undogmatic Christianity towards a propitiatory imitation of Christ in conduct. If it is likeness to Christ, especially in sacrifice, that commends us to God, instead of faith in Christ's sacrifice, then the difference between that and Romanism is only the difference between the ritual and the ethical expression of the same principle. Each makes really the same claim to God's favour through human action.

[1] 2 Cor. iv. 4. (R.V. *marg.*)

V

In many directions it appears that for the hour the religious world is more engaged with man's contribution to God than with God's contribution to man. This is the large interpretation of the sectional phenomenon of ritualism. We find it no less in the humanism than in the ethicism of the day. Erasmus, the earnest scholar, has taken the upper hand of Luther in the Christian tone of the prosperous educated hour. It is the spirit of Erasmus that rules educated society and colours the bench of bishops, who are scholars in Church history more than in the theology of Christian experience. They may not like the priest who takes himself thoroughly in earnest, but they have more sympathy with him than with the evangelical minister of the Word. To take extreme cases, they would probably find themselves more at home with the meticulous Laud than with the mighty Jonathan Edwards. They certainly are not able to cope, except by the aid or fear of the State, with the priest who does strive to realise the despair of human guilt and deal seriously with it. Whoever is to cope with the priest must follow him to the roots of human sin, only he must go deeper. A humanist reformation is little more than reform; it is not regeneration. And it is regeneration that the soul needs. But the Erasmic mind of the scholarly and pastoral clergyman misses the apostolic priesthood and ministry of the Word. His altar is much more than his pulpit, his every day is a day of trivial visitation, and he is more of a director of consciences than a prophet of the amazing, wrestling, living Word, which is hammer and fire upon the flinty rock of self-satisfaction. He tends to confessions more than conversions. And for the mending of the Church he would remove abuses, cherish a kindly, philanthropic Churchmanship, secure for the clergy a place midway between the Catholic and the Puritan with the force of neither, cultivate a reverence which is half æsthetic and good taste, soften dogma by ethical interpretations, and urge moral improvement in a spirit of not too much zeal. He does not gauge as even the literary man does the great human tragedy; he knows not the stung soul's exceeding bitter cry, nor does he thrill to the world's woe or the central chord of expiation on the cross. He is institutional even more than ethical, and ethical more than sympathetic or enthusiastic. He is quietly devout and subduedly active; but he has no burthen, and he does not compel them to come in by the native compulsion of the Gospel word. He has never truly reached the real marrow of Christian theology, the fundamental war of law and Gospel in the history of the soul.

VI

Again, ethical preoccupation leads in large numbers of "quiet people" to religious indifference, and religious indifference is the best soil for the priest. By religious indifference I mean the absence of personal concern and experience; I do not mean the lack of all interest in religious truths, institutions, or activities. In character and in philanthropy many stand high, and merit much, who are yet devoid of personal experience in the distinctive Christian sense of the word. There are those, even, who are entirely evangelical in their convictions, but their religion has never really passed beyond the region of truths; contact with a truth takes the place of commerce with a person. It should not be forgotten that the vicarious priesthood grew and flourished during those immature ages of the Church when right knowledge and good living were the sum of Christianity. And the new element in the Reformation which gave Christianity back to itself was the conviction that practical Christianity is not the plain man's pagan combination of certain authoritative views of God and the world with the practice of ethical virtues; but that it is the religious experience of trust in God's grace in Christ through faith, a faith which shapes the whole moral realm. There is, besides the absolute agnosticism of science, the relative and practical agnosticism of the excellent modest man who worships reverence more than confidence, and is a sound Churchman more than a true believer. It troubles him more to presume to know too much, than to shrink and trust too little. He is more afraid of pushing than he is of distrusting. He cherishes a vague hope of mercy, rather than a sure faith in grace. He hopes to be forgiven, rather than is sure that he is. He is bold in things honest, but most timid in things of faith. He is not so angry with the priest's claims as he is with the secret ways by which they are taught. There is that relative and even Christian agnosticism; and it may seem harsh to associate it with the more absolute and systematic—to mix up the man who knows no truth about God with the man who knows nothing but truth about God. But they are both strange to the real humility of Christian freedom and confidence in living faith. They are strange to direct and personal experience of God. And they are both types of mind too weak in the religious constitution to withstand attacks of the priest, chronic or acute.

VII

The temper of the hour is to a large extent priestly, because it is humanist, æsthetic, and Pelagian. Pelagianism was the temper of the medieval and scholastic Church which developed the priesthood, and the Reformers disowned it. We believe to-day in human nature, and the men of genius are its prophets. It is a liberal age, and the liberal, humane view of man is carried into religion till it ousts the soul. Like the medievals, we inhabit an æsthetic age. Faith is nowhere in the reading (or at least in the writing) world, and love is everywhere, love is enough. By this sentimental apparatus of the poetical *littérateur* the whole hoary world of spiritual problem is attacked and reduced with the masterly freshness of a young lady at the social board, who feels

> "The first that ever burst
> Into that silent sea."

And this literary apotheosis of love coincides with two tendencies in the interior of the Church itself. First, as Christian faith works out into love the children of the men of faith are more sensitive to love's atmosphere than to faith's. The grandchildren of the stalwart believers love their Christian homes and affections better than they understand the principles that reared them. They respond to the amenities of a cultured society better than they do to the vigour of Christian faith. They are more at home in a decorous and kindly Church than in a true. Cultured Protestantism itself loses the great evangelical note, and gravitates either to a feeble evangelism or to a Church of charm. And, secondly, the literary tendency falls in with the standing Catholic doctrine which puts love where the New Testament puts faith. So that Catholicism has the advantage and help of æsthetic Pelagianism on the one hand, and of the cultured piety of Protestantism on the other. Beautifying grace gets the better of justifying grace. And this is especially the case with women and with the young, who have a place in the Church they never had, at least in Protestantism, before. The fact is one which is here only noted and not deplored. It is all on the way to the promised land if only we do not think we have arrived.

VIII

Again, we must not overlook the welcome which the unspiritual man always gives to a religion which relieves him from spiritual effort, the very human belief in vicarious self-sacrifice and obedience by deputy. The separate, thaumaturgic, and dangerous character of the priesthood is due as much to the indolence of the laity as to the ambition of the clergy. It is the people that make the priests more than the priests make themselves. The vicarious priest flourishes on nothing so much as on public indifference. Canon Gore well points out how in the early Church the lowering of the average tone due to the rapid extension and secularising of the Church tended to throw up and isolate the ministry, to cast it together upon itself for sympathy, and to make it a spiritual aristocracy. And so to-day the claims made for the priest and his detachment from the layman are due, to no small extent, to the protest which an earnest spirituality must by its very existence make against the secularisation of religion in a Church which is at once the Church of the State and of the rich and fashionable.

IX

But after all other causes have been allowed for I continue to think that few are more favourable to priestly rule than that which I have first named, and which is all the more powerful because it is subtle enough to seem absurd. I allude to the popular passion for "doing things," which when imported into religion prepares a congenial welcome for the thaumaturgic priest. It is a temper which when uncurbed goes before to prepare a place for him in the Protestant mind itself. The real roots of the Roman reaction lie in the unrealised Romanism of Protestants. And the Protestant root of a mass priesthood is the idea so dear to the English mind, so central to a rational Broad Churchism in every Church, and so plausible as the ethical movement— the idea that the best action or conduct is contributory to salvation instead of produced by it. This is the Pelagian and Synergistic faith of medieval Catholicism reappearing in the circles of humanist Protestantism. Nothing is in more distinct contrast with the Protestant doctrine of justification by faith alone, nor in contrast more fatal. To adopt it is in principle to renounce the Reformation, whether it be done on agnostic or on Catholic lines. The Reformation had to break away for its life both from the Catholics and from the humanists. These, as I have said, took up Luther, but he outgrew them, as both Christ and Paul outgrew the humanist rabbis. It was not mere sacramental works that the Reformers denied to have saving value, but ethical no less. It was not the mere ritual of worship that Paul fought when he led Luther's way, but that of conduct as well. Man can contribute nothing to his own salvation. "Work out your own salvation, for it is God that worketh in you." Yes, but God the Redeemer; what works in you is the redemption which you have already apprehended by faith alone. The words were spoken not to the natural conscience but to the redeemed. Any form of Synergism is fatal to justification by grace alone, which is the base of true Protestant priesthood.[1]

---

[1] The most intractable of opponents are not the priests after all, but the ethical agnostics in the first place, and the merely ethical Christians in the second. The agnostic men of science at the

Christianity is a religion and a faith before it is an ethic. It is ethical because of its faith in the supreme and all-inclusive ethical act of God in the Redeemer.

The public mind, through the influence of a literary religion like Arnold's, has become deeply imbued with the idea that religion consists in behaving in a certain way, in doing something palpable, in belonging to the Church as "a society for the promotion of goodness," in heroic or pretty self-sacrifices, in morality tinged with emotion. And so the public, having this, as it might be called, ergistic habit of mind, is not startled as it should be by the vicarious doing of the priest; especially as there is a large class of people who, when a religious question is pushed beyond considerations of habit and decorum, being not so much indifferent as ignorant, give it up with the statement that they leave all that to their clergyman. The love of doing things becomes indifferent to the way they are done. And thousands prize as a badge of mental altitude and noble carelessness the shallow jingle—

"For forms of faith let graceless bigots fight ;
His can't be wrong whose life is in the right."

Moreover, along with the æsthetic and ethical move-

great centres of culture, if compelled to vote on an issue which involves the question of a Catholic form of Christianity or an evangelical, will vote for the Catholic, though it is the organization of all that they most deny.

ment has gone a social movement, submerging the individual and his responsibility in his organism, and accepting the acts of the society's representative or cleric as the unit's acts even when there is no continuity of faith or sentiment between them. The peril of specialized function, so great in these overbusy days, here appears in its religious form. The expert not only advises but replaces. Doing something is the condition of salvation, and it matters not that the doing is gone through by another so long as his credentials from the religious society are valid. When it is a case primarily of doing things, the condition of the doer is a minor matter, and the action easily passes from ethical to sacramental, and from that to hieratic; and the priest, ceasing to be a real representative through the circuitous remoteness of his connection with the living soul, easily becomes a substitute, and soon grows sole.

My point is that the most subtle, and for us the most perilous, departure from the New Testament and the Reformation is not in the priest who is express and positive in his claims. He is a symptom rather than a source. He would rouse our suspicion and alarm if it were not that we are got ready for him by a habit of public mind which opens the door from the inside. Our chief danger is the view and temper which makes that preparation and leaves the door ajar. It is the ethicism, practicism, ergism, nomism—call it concisely what you will—the conduct-worship and love of exploit which I have spoken of. This first takes up the debased idea of orthodoxy, that faith is belief in truths instead of Christ, and that unfaith, therefore, is the denial of certain truths; it goes on accordingly in a liberalising way to identify faith with the mere love of truth; it proceeds, very naturally and properly, to urge that such faith is inferior to action; it then, in its Pelagian and humanist fashion, replaces faith by either political and distributive justice, on the one hand, or by love, as the mere enthusiasm of humanity, on the other. These are its great motives and standards of action. And, throughout, it follows a debased and institutionalised Church in totally missing the true nature of faith as itself the supreme act, the initial and final surrender of the personality to the grace of God, the greatest and most compendious exertion of will of which man is capable, with all the integrities and humanities in its bosom. When the process has gone so far faith has ceased to be a matter of mere assent, and yet it has not become an act of will of the spiritual and decisive kind just described. The house is swept and garnished, but unoccupied still. And it is left open to the most attractive forms of action—ritual, ethical, or imaginative; to rites, conduct, or heroisms in their æsthetic aspect. And salvation is bound to become a thing either of admirable behaviour or of impressive ceremonial, if it is not to sink into the matter of sentiment which it has become in the feebler sects.

A religion of conduct tends to become a religion of ritual, because conduct is not religion and the appetite for "doing things" presses on to take a distinctly religious shape. If it do not find this in the true act of faith it finds it in what are called acts of faith, in sacraments as *opera operata*. If the idea of faith has been debased below the level of the soul's one decisive and inclusive act there is only left, to fill the really religious soul's passion for action, the sacramental path with a vicarious priest. If the spiritual answer to God's sole act be not in itself our central act then religion asserts its active nature by becoming contributory to God, instead of responsive. It becomes synergistic in the outward way, the ritual and imposing way (the ethical way not satisfying religious and imaginative need). And the ethical Church, the society for the promotion of goodness, is ground up between evangelical faith and Catholic sacraments, and its dust goes to the latter.

X

What we need, therefore, is a great rehabilitation of the idea and sense of faith among our Protestant selves, and not least among those sections of Protestants that cherish a rational and liberal creed. We need a renewal of practical religion in the sense of a New Testament revised and revived, in the sense of a personal experience whose centre and genius is guilt, grace and forgiveness. Sin is not, as the Greek idea of it goes, infection with a moral microbe; and salvation is not mere imparted $\alpha\phi\theta\alpha\rho\sigma\iota\alpha$, or incorruption. Nor is sin, as in the medieval idea, mere distance from God. It is what the Reformers declared it to be, guilt. That idea, grasped in its fulness and felt in its searching finality, was the great Reformation contribution to Christian faith. It made sin a religious besides a moral idea. The grace which saved from sin was not a sacramental infusion to counterwork an infused evil; it was the pure mercy of God exercised upon guilt and not injected against disease. Salvation was *sine merito redimi de peccatis.* That was the core of the Reformation. Sin became the idea that negatively coloured all, and prescribed the form of the positive faith that destroyed it. Redemption was the supreme humane interest, as it has now become, through Wagner, for humanism as art. It was faith not in the love of God but in the justifying grace of God, which in Christ received believing sinners as if they were not sinful, yet treated them as if they were, and by so dealing with them made them saints. Faith as the response to love may be Catholic; evangelical faith is the response to justifying grace, to the central act of the moral universe as a religious and a priestly act. It is this faith which, in whatever modified form, must revive in unmodified power. It is the only power that can save us from the priest, and without which no readjustment like Disestablishment can be of final use to religion. Agnostic science is a broken reed and a moral failure so long as it thinks the priest better for its wife and children and servants than the dreary negation it owns but cannot worship or trust at its own core.

True faith in an act like the cross, and in a person like Christ, must inevitably ethicise itself. Its nature, because of its object, is a spiritual ethic, universal, nay celestial, in its range, final and fundamental in its penetration of the soul. But it can only ethicise itself by remaining above all things absolutely religious. That is to say, the object of trust must be the last reality, the final object of knowledge and thought, the ultimate source, power, seat, and goal of things. Faith must be the answer to His self-revealed nature and character. It must be the response to a positive, final religion, and not the apotheosis of human religiosity. It has too readily accepted its moral corrections from the natural conscience, and made its appeal to the natural mind. It has taken over ideals and conclusions which it had not developed, and which do not represent its own genius. In Catholicism it did slowly what some Eastern nations have done more rapidly; it imported a civilization from the West ready made and full grown. As Japan takes Europe so young Christianity took the classical world. If it will return from the bondage of these ill-digested institutions, which it has served where it should have used—if it return from them to "readjust its compass at the cross" (as Goethe said), it will moralise and socialise itself at that source in a germane, distinctive and mighty way. But it is as dangerous for a weak and harassed faith to call in the literary or scientific ethics of the natural man as it is for a weak race to invite a strong one to its soil to help it against the perils its feebleness has caused. The mercenary force claims its conquest for payment. The guest stays on as virtual master, and the last state of that host is worse than the first. Faith at its own sources can throw off its own errors; it cannot be really corrected or supplemented by unfaith. "Religions," says Harnack, "cannot be skinned; we must cause them to scale" (*Dogmengesch.*, iii. 668). The fruit of the Spirit is often an act of oblivion. "Much is to learn and much to forget." To be taught of God is to unlearn much ; and to grow in grace is to cast off in the sun many wraps which the cold wind of mere criticism only blew the closer to our timid and benumbed souls.

www.ingramcontent.com/pod-product-compliance
Lightning Source LLC
Chambersburg PA
CBHW020810230426
43666CB00007B/943